BIRMINGHAM BREWERIES

Birmingham West Midlands England

Joseph McKenna

BREWIN BOOKS

© Joseph McKenna 2005

ISBN 1 85858 271 7

The moral right of the author has been asserted.

A Cataloguing in Publication Record
for this title is available from the British Library.

Typeset in Plantin
Printed in Great Britain by
Supaprint (Redditch) Limited
www.supaprint.com

CONTENTS

Acknowledgments..*VI*

Chapter 1   Early Brewers...*1*

Chapter 2   The Early Breweries..*5*

Chapter 3   Retail Brewers..*15*

Chapter 4   Victorian Breweries..*27*

Chapter 5   Takeovers & Mergers..*37*

Chapter 6   Up to the Millennium & Beyond..................................*39*

Chapter 7   A List of Birmingham Breweries, 1782-2002................*51*

Appendix I   The Tied Houses of Frederick Smith Ltd....................*90*

Appendix II   Who Took Over Who..*93*

Bibliography...*95*

Index..*96*

ACKNOWLEDGMENTS

My thanks to Paul Taylor and Andy "Bruce" Willis for their help.

For the Apprentice, who never knew the dark days of little choice and ten-thirty closing.

Chapter 1

EARLY BREWERS

The drinking of beer was essential at a time when water was sometimes dangerous to drink through impurity. The very nature of its production, the boiling of water and the fermentation into alcohol, ensured that beer was pure to drink – and remained so. Brewing was carried out in the home, and on the farm, usually by the woman of the house. At what date brewing was begun commercially in Birmingham is uncertain, but by 1166 its sale was regulated under the Market Charter granted by Henry II to Peter deBermingham. Of the Officers of the Manor, there were two Ale Conners, whose job was to ensure the quality of the beer sold, and the measures it was sold by. "The Powers and Officers of the Court Leet" was published in 1789, whereby the duties of the Ale Conners are clearly defined:

The Office of Ale Conners, otherwise High Tasters

"The Jury find and present, that these Officers are annually elected by the Jury; and their Duty is to see that all Publick Brewers and Ale Sellers within the Manor, do Brew good and Wholesome Drink, and that they do not Use in Ale or Beer any Guinea Pepper, Coculus, Judiac, or any other unwholesome or intoxicating Ingredients: and for the purposes of these Assays, the Officers may at seasonable Times, demand of each Publick Brewer or Ale Seller, a reasonable Quantity of his Ale or Beer, and which the Jury Estimate at half a Pint Ale Measure. And these Officers are to present all Publick Brewers and all Ale Sellers, selling or exposing to Sale bad and unwholesome Drink; and all common Tiplers and Drinkers, and all Alehouse-keepers permitting unlawful Tipling or Gaming in their Houses by Apprentices or others."

The two principal ingredients of early English ale, barley and water, were readily available in this north Warwickshire town. There was a Barley Lane in Birmingham by 1347, not far from "God Welle feld," off the present Edgbaston Street near the Bull Ring. This was the lane that led to the fields where barley was grown. Upper Digbeth High Street was alternatively known as Well Street, even as late as 1731, as is shown on William Westley's Plan of Birmingham for that year. Its name indicated the presence of numerous wells and springs. Water was still being extracted in large quantities from here, even as late as the Victorian period. The Digbeth Mineral Springs Company was established in 1854. Through an artesian bore, four inches in diameter, sunk 400 feet deep, 72,000 gallons of water was extracted each day.

Beer was available at the local ale-houses of the town, and also from the Priory, or Hospital of St. Thomas, situated in Chapel Street (now upper Bull Street). Brewing would have been carried out here, not only for the consumption of the monks, but also to supply travellers and pilgrims who found a night's accommodation here. The Priory was established in 1285 by Edward deBermingham. It was probably here at the Priory that one of the major innovations of brewing, the use of hops, was first introduced into the town by its Brewer monk. English ale at this time was brewed without the use of hops. They had been used on the Continent from the 11th Century onwards, but had met with resistance in England, though brewers had used a number of plants and herbs including rosemary, bog myrtle and yarrow, to counter the "biscuity" sweetness

BIRMINGHAM ALE.

YE lads and ye lasses come list to my lays,
   Attention too lend, while I Birmingham praise,
'Tis a place will be famous in after time story,
As adding a wreath to our National Glory.
          Derry down, &c.

For ALE are we famous, clear wholesome & strong,
One drop of it now would enliven my song.
Had my good Mother's milk tasted like it, I vow,
I ne'er would have left, but kept sucking 'till now.

Of GUY, Earl of Warwick, our country can boast,
Who in fighting & thumping rul'd lord of the roast
He with courage resistless his foes did assail,
For he strengthen'd his sinews with Birmingham Ale.

When he put on his armour to kill the Dun Cow,
Which he certainly did, tho' I can't tell you how,
He drank a full gallon of BIRMINGHAM ALE,
'Ere he ventur'd in battle to pull the Cow's tail.

Our swords & our guns thro' the world are the best
As our foes to their sorrow can truly attest;
With Birmingham Bayonets, Birmingham Ale,
No true British spirit was e'er known to fail.

Let each one that's true to our Town's honest fame
When he drinks of Ale mention Wellington's name
May be and his army Victorious prevail,
Ne'er want our roast beef or good Birmingham Ale.

Success to our lads who our credit maintain,
And win laurel wreaths with the heroes of Spain,
May they safely return--their sweethearts regale,
And relate all their dangers o'er Birmingham Ale.

Printed by S. TAYLOR, No. 112, Moor-street,
        Birmingham.
 , Books bound on the Lowest Terms.

Birmingham Ale, a ballad by John Freeth.

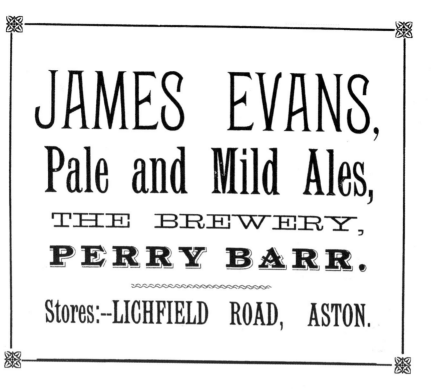

JAMES EVANS,
Pale and Mild Ales,
THE BREWERY,
PERRY BARR.
Stores:--LICHFIELD ROAD, ASTON.

James Evans, a retail brewer of Franchise Street.

of malted cereals. The hop added a bitterness to the beer, and a pleasing aroma. It also acted as a preservative that killed bacteria. It was not until the 16th Century however that hops in English beer became acceptable.

The Priory was closed down in 1547, during the Reformation, but by then a number of inns had been established in the town. Like the Priory they would have offered food, their own home-brewed beer, and accommodation for the night. Of these early inns there was the "Red Lion" in the Bull Ring, whose landlord in 1494 was Richard Mershall, the "Bull Inn" across the road from the Priory, the "Maiden Head" near St. Martin's Church, whose landlord in 1500 was John Cooper; the "Reindeer" in the High Street, "The Board" in Digbeth, "The Swan" at the junction of High Street and New Street, and the "White Hart" where famously in 1637, the Plague was last introduced to Birmingham by way of a bundle of clothes from London.

By the end of the 17th Century the pattern of brewing in London was changing. Innkeepers and alehouse brewers were being replaced by common brewers. Elsewhere throughout England the same thing was happening, but perhaps at a slower pace. To help them in their enterprises, a treatise, anonymously published in 1734 appeared. *The London and Country Brewer* offered advice to those taking up the venture new. It placed considerable emphasis on the clarity of beer, and its general appearance. It was important, for brewers now found themselves in a highly competitive market.

A "Triple A" advertisement for Ansells.

Chapter 2

THE EARLY BREWERIES

The first known brewery in Birmingham was opened in the Inkleys, off Hill Street, in 1752, but failed, according to The Pictorial Guide to Birmingham, published in 1849. There is no record of who set it up, the beer brewed, or when it closed. The second brewery was erected in 1782 by Joseph Ashton. It was situated at the junction of Moseley Street and Alcester Street, Deritend. Known simply as The Brewery, it became the Old Brewery when other breweries became established. In 1786 James Richards became a partner in the business. The building, situated on the edge of the then existing town, was purpose-built in brick. There are no illustrations of this early brewery, but A General Dictionary of Arts and Sciences published in 1765, offers some idea of its layout:

"In order to erect a large public brewhouse to the best advantage, several circumstances should be carefully observed. 1). That three sides in four of the upper part, or second floor, be built with wooden battons about three inches broad, and two thick, that a sufficient quantity of air may be admitted to the back of the coolers. 2). That the coppers be erected of a proper height above the mashing-stage, that hot water may be conveyed by means of cocks into the mash-tuns, and the worts into the coolers. 3). That the fire-places of the coppers be very near each other, that one stoker, or person who looks after the fire, may attend all. 4). That the yard of coals be as near as possible to the fire-places of the copper. 5). That the malt be ground near the mash tuns, and the mill erected high enough that the malt may be conveyed from the mill immediately into the mash tuns by means of a square wooden spout or gutter. 6). That the upper backs be not erected above thirty-three feet above the reservoir of water, that being the greatest height water can be raised by means of a common single pump. 7). That the pumps which raise the water, or liquor, as the brewers call it, out of the reservoir into the water-backs, and also those which raise the worts out of the jack back into the coppers, be placed so that they may worked by the horse-mid which grinds the malt."

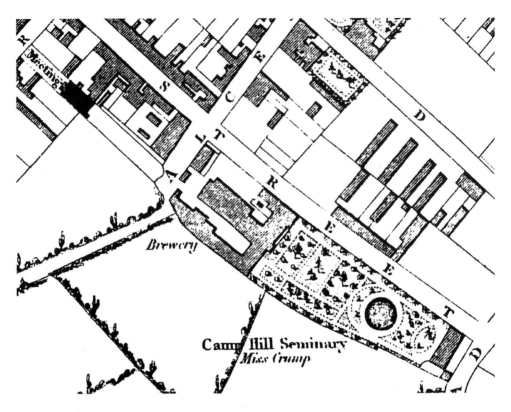

Plan of 1785 showing Ashton's Brewery, Deritend.

The third of Birmingham's breweries, was established to the north of the town at Warstone Lane, Hockley by John Giles & Co., in 1784. This brewery, eventually a 30 quarter, was supplied with water from a small rivulet that ran nearby. In *Pye's Directory* the firm is listed as "Ale and Porter Brewers." In the 18th Century there were three main types of beer brewed in England; an original brown or amber ale, akin to mild (seemingly brewed by Ashton & Richards), Porter and East India Pale Ale (I.P.A.).

Porter originated among the working class of London, and in particular porters – hence its name. It was their practice to drink a mixture of three different beers. Enterprising brewer, Ralph Harwood, it is claimed, combined the three into one called "Entire Butt" or "Harwood's Entire." It was a dark beer, almost black in colour, strong and well-hopped. After it was brewed, it was stored for a considerable time in huge vats to mature. In 1726 it sold for 3d. a pot.

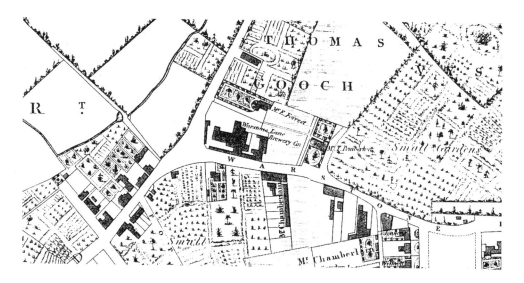

Plan of 1825 showing Forrest & Sons Warstone Brewery.

I.P.A. was the exact opposite. It is believed that it originated at the Bow Brewery in London, but was soon taken up by the brewers of Burton-on-Trent. It was light and sparkling, with a distinct slight bitter taste. It found its way to the dining table, as an alternative to wine, following the outbreak of the Napoleonic Wars. Its greatest market though was with the Far East, traded through the East India Company, hence its name.

The production of these very individual beers depended very much on the type of malt used. Barley was placed into a lead-lined or a tiled cistern that held five, ten, or more "quarters," and covered with water, filled to four or five inches above it, to allow for swelling. Then it was allowed to mature for five or six "tides." (reckoned to be twelve hours to the "tide."). The water was then drained, and the malt removed from the cistern.

It was laid out on the floor to dry. Drying times varied according to the season, from twelve to sixteen hours in warm weather to up to thirty hours in the cold. During this time the malt had to be constantly turned to prevent mould from growing. When dry the malt was placed in the kiln to roast, for four, or six, or twelve hours, according to the type of malt required. The pale required a cooler and more leisurely roasting than the amber or dark, which were roasted at a hotter temperature and for a shorter period. M. Combrune in his *Essay on Brewing*, published in 1758 sets out the temperatures required in Fahrenheit for producing different coloured malts:

WARSTONE-BREWERY. *Alex. Forrest, & Sons.*

The Warstone Brewery, an advert of 1800 from Pigot's Magnificent Directory.

Deg.
119 White
124 Cream Colour
129 Light Yellow
134 Amber Colour
138 High Amber
143 Pale Brown
148 Brown
152 High Brown
157 Brown inclined to black
162 High Brown, speckled with black
167 Blackish-brown with black specks
171 Colour of Burnt Coffee
176 Black

A view of the Birmingham Brewery, off Broad Street, 1815.

The brewing of these three distinctive beers also took into account different types of water used. Pale ale was brewed with either spring or common well water. Original or amber ales could be brewed with either hard or soft water, or indeed a mixture of both. Porter it was reckoned, was best brewed with river water, which in London came from the Thames or New River.

The first edition of the *Encyclopaedia Britannica; or a Dictionary of Arts and Sciences,* published in 1771, details how these three types of beer were brewed:

Stout Butt-beer or Porter.

"This is the strongest porter that is brewed from brown malt, and often sold for forty shillings the barrel, or six pounds the butt out of the wholesale cellars. The liquor in the copper designed for the first mash, has a two-bushel basket, or more, of the most hully malt thrown over it, to cover its top, and afterwards its boiling; this must

be made very hot, almost ready to boil, yet not so as to blister, for then it will be in too high a heat; but, as an indication of this, the foul part of the liquor will ascend, and the malt swell up, and then it must be parted, looked into, and felt with the finger or back of the hand, and if the liquor be clear, and of such heat as can be just endured, it is then enough, and the stoker must damp his fire as soon as possible, by throwing in a good parcel of fresh coals, and shutting his iron vent doors; immediately on this, they let as much cold liquor or water run into the copper as will make it all of a heat, somewhat more than blood-warm; this they pump over, or let it pass by a cock into an upright wooden square spout or trunk, and it directly rises through the holes of a false bottom into the malt, which is worked by several men with oars for about half an hour, and is called the first and stiff mash. While this is

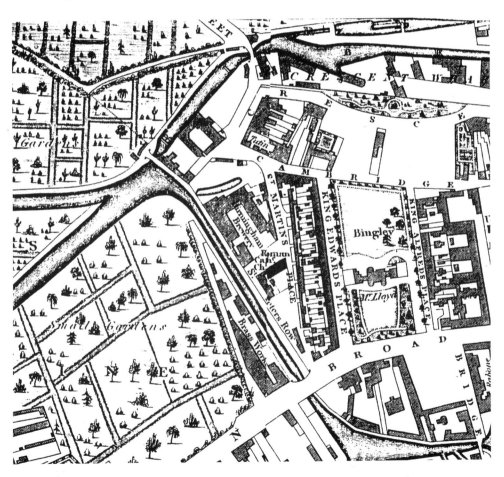

An early 19th Century map showing the Birmingham Brewery, off Broad Street.

Left. The Old Tree Inn, a home-brew house.
Right. Sales catalogue of the property of Charles Cox, brewer and maltster.

doing, there is more liquor heating in the copper, that must not be let into the mash tun till it is very sharp, almost ready to boil; with this they mash again, then cover it with several baskets of malt, and let it stand an hour before it runs into the under-back, which, when boiled an hour and a half with a good quantity of hops, makes this stout. The next is mashed with a cooler liquor, then a sharper, and the next blood-warm or quite cold; by which alternate degrees of heat, a quantity of small beer is made after the stout."

Common Brown Ale and Starting Beer.

"They take the liquors from the brown ale as for the stout, but draw a greater quantity from the malt than for stout; and after the stiff and second mash, they cap the goods with fresh malt, to keep in the spirit, and boil it an hour; after this, small beer is made of the same goods. Thus also the common brown starting butt-beer or porter is brewed, only boiled with more hops an hour and a half, and worked cooler and longer than the brown ale, and a shorter length drawn from the malt. But it is customary after the brown ale, or when a quantity of small beer is wanted, or is to be brewed better than ordinary, to put so much fresh malt on the goods as will answer that purpose."

Pale and Amber Ales and Beer.

"As the brown malts are brewed with river, these are brewed with well or spring-liquors. The liquors are by some taken sharper for pale than brown malts, and, after the first scalding liquor is put over, some lower the rest by degrees, to the last, which is quite cold, for their small beer; and for butt-beers, there is no other difference than the addition of more hops, and boiling, and the method of working."

Samuel Child, a brewer himself, in his *Every man His Own Brewer*, published in 1800, worked out the production costs of a number of different types of beer, including Porter. The costs below are for nine barrels:

Porter Receipt.	Average Expense £. s. d.		
One quarter of malt	2	2	0
8lb. hops	0	9	4
9lb. treacle	0	1	6
8lb. liquorice root	0	5	4
8lb. essentia bina	0	4	8
8lb. colour	0	4	8
Capsicum ½ oz.	0	0	2
Spanish liquorice 10 oz.	0	0	1
Cocculus Indicus, commonly called Occulus India berries, ¼ oz.	0	0	2
Salt of tartar 2 drachms.	0	0	1
Heading ¼ oz.	0	0	1
Ginger 3 oz.	0	0	3
Lime, 4 oz. Slacked, and the water. After having received the spirit of the lime, poured into the essentia bina, or colour, in making	0	0	1
Linseed 1 oz.	0	0	0½
Cinnamon 2 drachms.	0	0	1½
	3	8	7
Coals	0	2	9
Total	£. 3	11	4

Joseph Ashton died in 1787.Now a man of note, his obituary appeared in the daily newspaper, *Aris's Gazette*. Richards continued on until his own death, on 28th April 1799. He was succeeded by his son, who took James Goddington on as a partner. By 1817 four breweries had sprung up in Birmingham, Messers Richards & Co., formerly Richards & Goddington in Deritend, Forrest & Sons in Warstone Lane, the Britannia Brewery off New Town Row, and the Union Brewery just off Broad Street. The Britannia was the largest brewery of its kind outside of London, according to Jabet's *Concise History of Birmingham,* published in 1808. Its life was short however, and by 1819, it had been converted into a nail manufactory.

The Union Brewery was established in Saint Peter's Row, just off Broad Street in 1807, where some eighty years later William Butler built his Crown Brewery. In 1814 the Union Brewery was taken over by a consortium of gentlemen including the Quaker banker, Samuel Lloyd. Coincidentally a few years earlier, family member David Lloyd in partnership with William Summerfield, had founded the Coventry Brewery. The Union Brewery was renamed the Birmingham Brewery, and over the next 120 years had a variety of owners and names. From 1821-29 it was Horton and Smith's Broad Street Brewery, during the 1840s it was run by Breidenback, Johnston and Howell, and later Howell, Rooke, Cooper and Grigg. Throughout the 1860s it was Cooper and Grigg. A Grigg descendant incidentally, Henry Grigg, later went on to form the Grigg & Brettell Brewery in Kyrwick's Lane, Sparkbrook, in 1895. During the 1870s the Birmingham Brewery was run by Cooper & Co., and later during that decade became the Birmingham & District Brewery Co. The brewery closed in 1882, and its buildings were leased out as warehouse space.

In 1830 the Duke of Wellington's Beerhouse Act abolished duty on beer and made it possible for any householder who could afford two guineas, to buy a licence to sell beer. This saw the advent of the retail brewer. Their function seems akin to the modern day off-licence. The beer was brewed on the premises, in a small brewhouse, and sold directly to the customer in small measures. The geographical spread of these retailers particularly in the early 19th Century, covered much of the then existing town and its suburbs. Each brewer it would seem, supplied their immediate neighbourhood. Between 1828 and 1830, both *Pigot & Co.'s National and Commercial Directory of Warwickshire,* and *West's Directory for Warwickshire,* list these retail brewers, showing it to be a growing enterprise. One hundred and sixteen retail brewers are listed during this period. Just over ten per cent of these brewers were women, following what was traditionally women's work. Some of the male retail brewers had dual-occupations. John Hoffmeyer for instance, a native of Berlin, was also a clockmaker. Below are listed those one hundred and fifteen retailers listed by Pigot and West during this period, plus those individuals entered in later directories, thus giving a more complete picture of the retail brewing trade. Some of these brewers opened home brew public houses, and where known, have been transferred to the main list of brewers.

Home-brewed ales by George Griffin of the Slaters Arms.

Chapter 3

RETAIL BREWERS

Adcock, Mrs., Livery Street, 1850.
"Joseph Matthews, brewer to Mrs Adcock of Livery Street, aged 65, died 25th January 1850." (*Aris's Gazette*, 28th Jan. 1850).

Alexander, Perry & Co., 4, Upper Priory, 1871.

Allen, Thomas, 24, Floodgate Street, 1854.

Allin [or Allen], William, 3, Brewery Street, off Newtown Row. (1828-30).

Allsop & Burke, Bridge Street West, 1852-3.

Andrews, Abraham, 100, Lupin Street, 1865.

Anyon, Thomas, 32, Nova Scotia Street, off Coleshill Street. 1828-30.
In 1830 the brewery was being run by Joseph Anyon.

Archer, George, Newdigate Street, Nechells, 1892.

Archer, Henry, 47½, Brewery Street, 1854.

Archer, Joseph, 150, Spring Hill, 1871.

Armstrong, Thomas, 118, Moseley Street, Deritend, 1828-30.
Situated not very far away from Joseph Ashton's original wholesale brewery.

Ashford, Joseph, 10, Aston Lane, East, 1882.

Ashford, Thomas, New Canal Street, off Meriden Street, Digbeth. 1829.

Atkinson, W.O., 167, Church Road, 1882

Avrill, William, 132, Moseley Street. 1829-30. Not far from Thomas Armstrong's retail brewery at No. 118.

Ball, George, Palmer Street, Bordesley. 1829.

Bartlom, W., Cheapside, Digbeth, 1845.

Barton, George Henry, 342, Arthur Street, Small Heath, 1901-12.

Bellamy, Ann, 6, Sun Street, off Bristol Street. 1829.

Bentley, Henry & Co. Ltd., 51-52, Pinfold Street, 1883.

Benton, Richard, 39, Barford Street, off Bradford Street, Deritend, 1829.

Berry, Thomas, & Co., 105, Digbeth,1871-7.

Bigford, John, Sherborne Street, 1877.

Bigford, Richard, Bromsgrove Street, 1843.

Bland, William, 228, Bristol Street. 1829.

Blizard & Colman, 7, Castle Street, 44, Meriden Street and Tewkesbury, 1869-70. John Leek, agent.

Bloxham, John, Bordesley Street, 1843.

Bolton, James, Cecil Street, Newtown. 1829.

Bomford, Ernest, 16, Temple Street, 1899.

Booth, Edward, Lawley Street, 1830.

Booth, Walter, 14, Cato Street, 1871.

Bott, W.C., 41, High Street, Deritend, 1902.

Bradbury, Alfred, 70, Victoria Road, Aston, maltster and brewer, declared bankrupt in August 1880.

Bridgens, J., 138, Scholefield Road, 1860

Broad, Richard, Branstone Street, 1882.

Bromford, Ernest, 16, Temple Street, 1898.

Brooks, George, 291, Cheapside, Digbeth, 1829.

Brown, J.C., Camp Hill, 1866.

Brown, Joseph, Cato Street, 1872.

Brown, Thomas, 95, Park Street, 1854.

Buckley, John, 110, Gib Heath, 1854.

Buckley, John Joseph, 315, Park Road, Hockley, 1875. 412, Park Road in 1883. In 1886, the brewery was extended into 414, Park Road. In 1888 Mrs Phoebe Buckley, presumably J.J.'s widow, was running the business.
Last directory entry is in 1895.

Bull, Richard, 262, Bradford Street, 1841-2.

Carr, Richard, Cato Street North, Nechells, 1867-9.

Carter, James, 40, Oxford Street, Digbeth. 1829-30.

Charlesworth, J., 5 Court, Moseley Street, 1854.

Chatwin, Samuel, 47, Ellis Street, off Holloway Head, 1829.

Cheshire, Evan, 5, Freeman Street, 1854.

Cheshire, William, 26, Cannon Street, 1852-3.

Clarke, Robert, Warwick Street, Bordesley. 1829.

Clarke, Samuel, 68, Summer Lane, Newtown. 1829.

Clements & Berry, 44, Meriden Street, Digbeth. 1866. Stores, 105, Digbeth & 44, Meriden Street, 1867. Last entry, 1870.

Cliff, George Griffin, Perry Barr, 1877.

Clulo, James, 138-139, Scholefield Street, 1870.

Cole, Samuel, Sandpits, 1852-3.

Collins, John, Mill Street, Islington, off Five Ways. 1829.

Colson, S., 13, Vauxhall Grove, 1866.

Combe & Co. Ltd., 125, Benacre Street, Balsall Heath, 1897.
51, Sherbourne Road in 1899.

Cookes, William, Windmill Street, off Holloway Head, 1886-92.

Cooksley, James, 15, Key Hill, 1870.

Cooper, Thomas, Perry Barr, 1860.

Cooper, Thomas & Co., 105, Digbeth, 1881-90. 1, Cannon Street.
Thomas Parsons agent. 1892-5

Corbett, John, 22, Upper Gough Street, off Suffolk Street. 1829.

Corn, James, Great Barr Street, Bordesley. 1828-30. This small brewery
may also have supplied additional beer to Joseph Brownell's nearby public
house, the *King's Arms.*

Cotterill, Ernest William, 193, Bristol Street, 1878-83.

Cotton, William Thomas, 71, Hampton Street, 1876.

Cowley, A., 48, Smith Street, Great Hampton Row, 1864.

Cox, Charles, *Parliament House,* 39, Ashted Row, 1875-85. *Woodman Inn,*
Well Street, Hockley. 1883-5

Cox, James, 52, Bradford Street, 1839.

Currier, J., Lawrence Street, 1854.
"Mary Jane Currier, wife of J. Currier, retail brewer, Lawrence Street,
aged 48. Died 3rd Feb. 1854." (*Aris's Gazette,* 6th Feb. 1854).

Darrall, James, Barr Street, Hockley. 1829.

Darrall, Robert, Newtown Row, 1829-30. Possibly related to James Darrall
listed above.

Dauncey, Mrs Laura, 192, Great Lister Street, 1895.

Davenport, Alfred, 25, Hick Street, Highgate, 1875-81.

Davenport, James, 118, Hospital Street, 1860-82 & maltster.

Davenport, Robert, 120, Brearley Street, 1829.
See also **Davenports Brewery.**

Davenport, Robert, 42, Princes Street, 1829, and Pritchett Street,
off Aston Road, in 1830. There is obviously some family connection with
the Robert listed above.

Dawes, Thomas, Moat Row, near St. Martin's Church. 1830.

Dawson, Popplewell, & Co., New Canal Street, 1882. Dawson & Co.,
1883-94.

Deakin, Joseph, Pritchett Street, 1829. It seems probable that he is the
"Joseph Dakin" of Pritchett Street, listed in *West's Directory* of the
following year.

Devonport, George, *White Swan,* 118, Hospital Street, 1876.

Doling, George, 11, Masshouse Lane, 1829.

Dutton, John, Palmer Street, Bordesley, 1829.

Edkins, David, Moor Street, 1830. See also **Edkins & Guy** in main listing.

Edkins, John, 52, Great Barr Street, 1854.

Edmonds, Richard, Livery Street, 1830.

Edwards, John, Heneage Street, Gosta Green, 1829.

Elcocks, William, Dartmouth Street, 1829. There is a second entry for
    a William Elcocks at nearby Leicester Place, Aston Road, that same year.
    Possibly the same man or near relative.

Ellington, Edward, 82, Bradford Street, 1867-72.

Elton, Edward, See: **Highgate Brewery.**

Elton, John, 138-139, Scholefield Road, 1892-4.

England, G. J., Castle Street, High Street, 1862-6.

Evans, Edgar, Wellhead Lane, Perry Barr, 1878. See also: **Well Head
    Brewery.**

Evans, James, Franchise Street, Perry Barr, 1888-98. In 1899 he opened a
    further premise at 228, Lichfield Road. 1900.

Evans, Thomas, 86, Hurst Street, 1871-80.

Evans, W., 138, Scholefield Street, Great Lister street, 1864.

Eyre, Sarah, 4, Upper Priory, 1858. Mole & Mander, agents.

Faulkner Brothers, (Botanical). 34, Runcorn Road, Moseley 1926-36.

Farmer, Nehemiah, Bordesley Street, 1830.

Fellows, Joseph, Stoney Lane, 1869.

Fincher Brothers, Gower Street, Lozells, 1888-90.

Fisher, J., 54, Key Hill, 1845.

Fletcher, James, Key Hill, 1843.

Flinn & Co., Ninevah Road, Handsworth, 1875-99. See also:
Handsworth Brewery.

Foster & Co., 258, Lichfield Road, 1882.

Freeman, George, Warwick Road, Acocks Green, 1872-84.
    Henry Freeman, Warwick Road, Acocks Green, 1885-7.

Fulford, Henry, Acocks Green, 1875-6.

Fulford, John, 14, Bloomsbury, 1878-9.

Galton, C. & Co., Moor St., 1882.

Garton, Charles & Co., Moor Street, 1878-8. Curzon Hall,
    Suffolk Street, 1884-90.

Griffin, George, *Slaters Arms,* 38, Rushton Street, 1892-5. "Families & the
    trade supplied."

Guardner, H.S., 21, Holloway Head. 1892.

Guille, William, Nursery Tce., Hunter's Lane, 1871-2. There may possibly be some connection with **Hockley Brewery.**

Gibson, Richard Charles, 168, Icknield Street East, 1866-77.

Gilbert, T., 222, Watery Lane, 1866.

Gill, Joseph, Hunter's Lane, Hockley. 1829. Some four years later Cox & White opened their Hockley Brewery a few doors down.

Glascote, Elizabeth, New Canal Street, Digbeth, 1830.

Green, James, Garrison Lane, 1854.

Greensill, Jonathan Peter, 109, Heneage Street, 1841-2. In 1844 Greensill moved to 81, Aston Street.

Greensill & Marston, Bordesley Street and Rea Street, 1852-3. Probably J.P. Greensill above.

Griffiths, John & Arthur, 43, Whittall Street, 1868. Whittall Street and 105, Newhall Street. Alfred Peyton, agent. Griffith, J.A. & Co., 1870.

Hackney, John, Lozells Lane, Aston, 1829.

Hall, Henry, Floodgate Street, Deritend. 1829-30.

Halford, W. & Son, 58, Aston Road; 44, Mill Street & 36, Holt Street, 1888.

Hall & Co., Albert Street, Dale End, 1872.

Hancocks, William, 39, Highgate Street, 1876-7.

Hands, John, Bertholem Street, 1854. An unknown road. Hands is listed in *Shalders' Birmingham Directory* for 1854.

Harons, Charles, 32, Milk Street, 1854.

Harcourt, Edward, 50, Smallbrook Street, 1852-4.

Harraman, William, Warwick Street, which runs parallel to Bordesley High Street, 1828.

Harrison, John, 23, Legge Street, Gosta Green, 1829-30.

Harrison, Sarah, 47, William Street, off Islington Row, Five Ways. 1828-30.

Hasip, Frederick, 22, Camden Street, Parade, 1880.

Hatton, Benjamin, Lawley Street, Duddeston, 1829.

Hatton, Martha, 68, Bath Street, 1829.

Hawley, John, 53, Mill Lane, off Digbeth High Street, 1829.

Hemming, George, 193, Bristol Street, Edgbaston Street, 108, Upper Trinity Street & Park Lane, Park Street, 1871-2. & Smithfield Passage, 1875-6. 1877-83. 110, Bristol Street, 1884-6. George Hemmings & Sons, **West End Brewery,** Bristol Street, 1888. Last entry, 1890.

Henson, Albert, 1, High Park Street, Nechells, 1886.

Herbert, William, Brighton Road, Balsall Heath, 1869.

Hicken, W., 100, Bath Row, 1860-4.

Hill, William, 47, Court, Cheapside, 1854.

Hillman, Sophia, Pritchitt Street, 1828-9.

Hipkiss, James, 12, Well Street, Digbeth, 1864-6. 11 & 12, Well Street, 1867-80,

Hodges, J., 22, Bishop Street South, 1867.

Hodgkins, Edward, 9 & 11, Johnstone Street, 1882. There may be some sort of tie-in with Birchfield Brewery.

Hodson, Edward, 18, Bagot Street, off Newtown Row, 1829.

Hodson, James, 39, Lower Tower Street, off Summer Lane, 1829. The following year he is listed at Tower Street, though this may be the same premises.

Hoffmeyer, John, Great Charles Street, 1830. Also a wooden clock maker.

Holden, William, 23, New Summer Street, off New Town Row, 1829-30. (Bristol Street).

Holleyoake, John, 228, Bristol Street, 1882.

Hollins, William, 10, Sheepcote Street, 1854.

Hollister & Smith, Grosvenor Road, Handsworth, 1863.

Holmes, John, Coventry Street, 1866.

Hopcroft, Alfred, 15, Frederick Street, Graham Street, Birmingham, and at Brackley and Banbury, 1867. 1868: 15, Frederick Street and Graham Street.

Hope, John, Witton Lane, 1876-7.

Horsfall, C., 255, Green Lane, Small Heath, 1902.

Hubbard, William, Palmer Street, Bordesley, 1829.

Hudson, William, 118, Bordesley Street, 1882.

Hughes, Thomas, 16, Lawrence Street, 1866.

Hunt, William, 57, Newhall Street, 1854. 84, Newhall Street, 1855-77.

Hunt & Co., Castle Street, 1869. & Uttoxeter.

Hutton Brothers, offices & stores, 4, Rea Street, 1888-90.
   See also: **Hutton's Brewery.**

Jackson, Henry, Bell Street, 1854.

James, Robert, 71, Villa Street, Handsworth, 1881.

Jameson, Pim & Co., 4, Upper Priory, 1866. 44, Meriden Street, 1875-6. Thomas Parsons, agent. 1879-84. 21, Castle Street, until 1888.

Job, Edward, Bartholomew Street, 1830.

Jones, David, 60, Tennant Street, off Islington Row, 1829.

Jones, G. Kingston Brewery, Adderley Street, 1902.

Jones, George, 100, Watery Lane, 1899-1904. 1905: George William Jones. 1906-17.

Jones, John, 164, Gooch Street, 1866. John Jones & Co., 84, Newhall Street, and in 1878 is listed as John P. Jones, of 84, Newhall Street.

Jones, William, Claremont Cottage, Red Hill, Yardley, 1872.

Joyner, Thomas, 4, Coventry Street, off Digbeth High Street, 1829.

Judd, John, & Co., 87-90, Coleshill Street, 1868.

King & Barton, Wrentham Street, 1903-11. Taken over by **Ansells.**

Kingston, James, Wharf Street, 1855.

Kinsman, Samuel, 29, Ward Street, New Town, 1829.

Knight, Thomas, New Road, Handsworth, 1829.

Knowles, Thomas, Lower Trinity Street, Deritend, 1829.

Lea, John & Sons, Balsall Heath Road, 1902. 81, Highgate Road, 1913-17.

Lea, Robert, Priestley Road, Sparkbrook, 1899-1900.

Leedham, William, 68, Bath Street, off lower Snow Hill, 1828-30.

Lightwood, John, 94, Summer Lane, 1829.

Lingard, William, 73, Snow Hill, 1829-30.

Long, Charles, 2, Clarendon Street, Aston New Town, 1883-95.

Lowe, Edward, 27, Nelson Street, 1854.

Lucas, Blackwell & Arkwright, 94, New Street, 1886-94. Also 5, Ethel Street from 1892.

Lunn, Joseph, 6, Mary Ann Street, 1868-72. William Lunn, 1875-8.

Manders, Robert & Co., 43, Meriden Street, 1876-7. Richard Milligan, agent. From 1880-83, at 21, Castle Street.

Mansfield, Thomas & Miss Ann Maria, Yardley Road, Acocks Green, 1900-23.

Manton, Robert, *Pelican Inn,* 54, Dymoke Street. Brewer and beer retailer, declared Bankrupt in December 1881.

Marrian, William, 14, Moseley Street, 1830.
Most probably has a connection with the Marrian, of **Marrian & Crockler's Heneage Street Brewery.** In 1833 a William Marrian of 74, Moseley Street, is listed as a brewer to the **Warstone Brewery.**

Martin, John, Aston Road, 1829.

Matthews, Richard, Coventry Road, Hay Mills, 1904-8. Forrest Road, Hay Mills, 1909-12.

Matthews, William, Preston Street, Bloomsbury, 1870.

Maule, Carteret, Brewery Street, Handsworth, 1894-7.

Mayo, Arthur, 75, Warwick Street, Deritend, 1900-2.

Mealing & Co., Gower Street, Lozells, 1892.

Middleton, Edward, 56 & 57, Legge Street, Aston Road, 1866-76. Chester Road, New Oscott from 1872-1902. Middleton, Edward jr., 57, Legge Street, 1878-94.

Millichamp, Joseph, Pritchett Street, 1830.

Mills, William, Lawley Street,1828-30. There is a second William Mills listed at Walmer Lane for 1829.

Moore, Jonathan, 9, Communication Row, Islington, 1829.

Moore & Simpson, Priory Road, Aston, 1890. Aston Lane in 1892. & Priory Road, Aston in 1894. Directory entries until 1907.

Morgan, T. Bradford Street, 1843.

Morton, H., 163, Vaughton Street, 1902.

Muggleton, Thomas Henry, 137, Bloomsbury Street,1894.

Nash, James, Hockley Hill, 1828-30.

Neal, James, 390, Lichfield Road, 1876-81.

Neville, James, 76, Moland Street, Gosta Green, 1829-30.

New, John, 122, Lee Bank Road, 1876.

Newey, Samuel, 149, New John Street West, 1882.

Newman, James & Son, 47, Arthur Street, Small Heath, 1900. 1902: M.E. Newman. 1903: James Newman & Son again. In 1905 Mrs Mary E. Newman. 1906-12

Newton, Thomas, Ashted Row, 1830.

Nichols & Stone, 31, Paradise Street,1868.

Non-Deposit Beer Co. Ltd., 69a, Bath Row, 1900-1.

Norton, William Henry, Crescent Bridge, near Farmer's locks. 1829. Probably servicing the narrow boat trade. In the following year Charles Norton is listed as the proprietor.

Overton, J., Nelson Street West, 1866.

Owen, John, 137, Bloomsbury Street, 1897.

Pagett, Walter, 17b, Moat Lane, 1894-5.

Palmer, William, 110, Bordesley Street, 1854.

Parkes, Richard, 9, Cherry Street. 1828-30.

Parmenter, John, 2, Victoria Place, Sandpits. 1846-50.

Payton, John, 94, Pope Street, near Five Ways, 1829.

Payton, Joseph, Broad Street, 1829. His brewhouse was not too far away from **Simcox & Ainsworth's** wholesale brewery in St. Martin's Place.

Pearman, Thomas, 94, Great Hampton Street, 1829.

Peden, Alex., 37, Lichfield Road, 1882.

Penny, Thomas, 73, Park Street and Brook Street. 1828-30. "Thomas Penny, retail brewer of New John Street West, aged 45, died 17th Dec. 1847." (*Aris's Gazette* 27th Dec. 1847).

Perkins, Joseph, 31, Bromsgrove Street. 1828-30.

Perks, William S. & John, 109½, New Street, 1852-8. Robert Thornley is listed as their agent.

Perry, Edward, Hospital Street, off Summer Lane, 1829.

Perry, Robinson, G., &Co., 4, Upper Priory, 1872.

Pettipher, Adam Prattingham, 30, Heath Street, 1870.

Phillips, John, Eyre Street, Spring Hill, 1829.

Phillips Brothers, Corn Exchange entrance, Castle Street, 1872.

Pickering, William, Anchor Brewery, 125, Park Road, Aston, 1902.

Piddington, Charles, 8 & 9, Ludgate Hill, 1876.

Pinchin, George & Co., 41, Cannon Street, 1858.

Powers, Thomas, 133, King Edward's Road 1871.

Price, W.A. & Co., Wellington Road, Handsworth, 1912.

Proctor, W., Coventry Road, Hay Mills, 1902. Took over the White Swan Brewery in Barwick Street in 1904. A home-brew house, fronting onto Edmund Street. Last directory entry is in 1923.

Quayle, Thomas, 157, Tennant Street, 1868.

Ratcliff, William, 24, Great Hampton Street, 1860. The following year his brewhouse had been renamed the Coventry Ale Stores. Closed (?)1863.

Rawlins, Mark, 244, Heneage Street, 1876.

Raworth, William, Lawley Street. 1828. The following year his address is given as Belmont Village, which appears to be the Lawley Street area, off Belmont Row, just north of Curzon Street.

Reay, William, Lawley Street, 1829.

Reeves, Thomas, 3, Meriden Street, 1882.

Reynolds, Sarah, 105, Great Hampton Street, 1829. Just across the road from Thomas Pearman's brewhouse.

Richards, John, 94, Camden Street, Springfield, 1895.

Richardson, Joseph, 2, Woodcock Street, Gosta Green, 1829.

Robinson, Samuel, Newtown Row, 1829. The following year his address is given as Lancaster Street, a street that continues on from Newtown Row. Probably confusion over the same address.

Rodway, James B., 24, Hagley Road, 1860-3.

Rooke, Joseph, Birchfield, 1850.

Rose, Edward, 55, Bishopgate Street, near Five Ways, 1829.

Rose & Hollis, 217-218, Icknield Port Road, Edgbaston, 1894-1901.

Rotton, George, 1, Adelaide Street, 1881.

Rudder, C.J., 28, Sutherland Street, 1902.

Sanderson, A. & Co., Brewery Street, Handsworth, 1883-92.

Sandiford, James, 42, Nechells Park Road, 1882.

Sargant, Isaac Henry, Stirchley Street, King's Norton, 1875-6.

Sa[u]nders, Edward, 27, St. James' Place, Vauxhall Road, 1882.

Savatard, A., 381, Nechells Park Road, 1882.

Saxon, Thomas & Co., (botanical). 123a, Balsall Heath Road, 1911-33.

Seaton, Richard, 15, Communication Row, 1875-6.

Seymour & Cliff, Perry Barr, 1875-6.

Skrine, George, Ashted Row, 1829.

Sloane, Michael, Franchise Street, Perry Barr, 1877.

Small, William H., 533, Bordesley Green, 1908.

Smalley, J., 68, Great Francis Street, 1860.

Smith, Elizabeth, 32, Adderley Street, Deritend, 1829.

Smith, Frederick C., 55, Spring Hill, 1855-8.

Smith, Henry, 87, New Canal Street, 1829. There was a second Henry Smith at 118, Cheapside, Digbeth.

Smith, J., 88, Suffolk Street, 1845.

Smith, James, 7, Lozells Road, Aston. 1876-7.

Smith, John, 117, Lionel Street, 1876.

Smith, Joseph, 49, Great Russell Street, 1862. 348, New John Street West, 1871-86.

Smith, Samuel, Summer Lane, 1830. There is a second Samuel Smith listed in Lawley Street at the same time.

Smith, W.M., Spring Hill, 1843.

Smith, William, Rea Street, Deritend. 1828-30.

Smith, William, 25, Aston Lane, Aston, 1879.

Smith & Savage, 27 & 28, Duke Street, 1904-10.

Smout, Henry, Warley Road, Hagley Road, 1881.

Southan, Richard, 47, Edmund Street, 1829.

Sparrow, M. 87, New Canal Street, 1902.

Spencer, John, New Canal Street, 1830.

Spooner, Harold & Co. (botanical), 81, Warwick Road, Sparkhill, 1911-16.

Standley, William, 48, Barford Street, off Moseley Street. 1828.

Stanton, Francis, 123, Ashted Row, 1854.

Steedman, Joseph, 121, Bath Row, 1845-48. Brewer and maltster. Premises bought by John and Edward **Davenport** in 1849.

Stenson, Joseph, 55, Erskine Street, 1882.

Stephens, Richard Gardener, 171, Somerset Road, Handsworth, 1905.

Stinson, George, Vauxhall Lane, Duddeston. 1828-30.

Stokes, Edwin, 74, Pershore Street, 1854-61.

Stone, John, 92, Ryland Road, 1882. & 58, (back of) New John Street, (1883-1906) See: **Anchor Brewery.**

Street, George, 78, Carver Street, 1871.
Swift, Thomas, 15, Francis Street, 1882.
Tabberner, Thomas, 31, Bromsgrove Street, 1829.
Taylor, Thomas, Factory Road, 1854.
Taylor, William, 26, Duke Street, Gosta Green, 1829.
Thomas, John, Newdigate Street, 1894-5.
Thompson, John & Sons, 2, Digbeth & 2a, Summer Row, 1875-9.
    1880 George Edwin Hunt, manager. 10, Summer Row in 1881.
Thompson, Robert, Groves' Buildings, Summer Lane, 1829.
Thompson, Samuel & Sons, 4 & 5, Carrs Lane, 1882.
Timms, George, 204, Cromwell Street, 1886-90.
Tisdale, Thomas, Wrentham Street, 1854.
Tongue, Henry, 77, Hockley Street, 1850.
Thrupp, R., Birchfield, 1845.
Truman, Henry, 29, Edmund Street, 1829.
Truman, Hanbury, Buxton & Co., Slaney Street, 1880.
Tunsell, George, Vauxhall Lane, 1830.
Turner, Clary Ann, 30, Cherry Street, 1829.
Turner, Maria, Manchester Street, off New Town Row, 1830.
Twigg, Samuel, 75, Lombard Street, 1829.
Twist, Richard, Great Barr Street, Bordesley, 1829-30.
Umfreville, J., 59, Graham Street, near St. Paul's Church, 1845.
Walford, W., Smithfield and Wolverhampton, 1845.
Walker & Son, Birchfield, 1860-3. Walker, William, 3, Johnstone Street,
    Birchfield, 1883.
Ward, Elizabeth, 48, Bradford Street, 1829.
Warner, Walter, 72, Bloomsbury Street, 1895.
Watkins, Charles & Son, 20, Aston Street, 1895-8.
Watson, Robert, Walmer Lane, 1829.
Watson, William, Duke Street, off Gosta Green. 1828-30.
Watts, Joseph, 9, Sheepcote Lane, 1854.
Watts & Co., 4, Rea Street, Deritend, 1882. G. Baker, agent.
Webb, Frederick, Angelina Street 1888.
Webb, William, 63, Hospital Street, 1829.
Webster, J., 56, Digbeth, 1902.
Welch, George, 8, Little Charles Street, 1855-8.
Weller, Thomas, 143, Great Tindall Street, Balsall Heath, 1875-86.
Wells, Joseph, 32, Cherry Street, 1842.
Whatney, Mary, "top of Clive Street", 1829.

While, Thomas, 36, Henrietta Street, near St. Paul's Church on the
Colmore Estate, 1829.

Whinwood, Henry, Stoke Street, 1854.

White, Job, 137, Bloomsbury Street, 1895.

White & Lake, 1, Wrentham Street, 1897.

Whitehouse, William, 30, Charlotte Street, off Newhall Street, 1829.

Williams, William, 54, Factory Road, (1854). 23, Kenyon Street, 1890-2.

Willitts, William, 63, Great Hampton Row, 1829.

Wilson, John, 336, Cheapside, Digbeth, 1829.

Wilson, John, 103, Pritchett Street, 1875-6.

Winn, William Aulton, 1, Legge Street, Gosta Green, 1829.

Wood, Alice, 101, Dale End. 1828-30.

Wood, Sarah, 106, New John Street, 1829-30.

Woodward, George, 18, Yates Street, Aston, 1892.

Wright, Jeremiah, Summer Lane, 1830.

Yeomans & Thacker, Gib Heath, 1845.

Young, Herbert, Great Brook Street, Ashted. 1828-30.

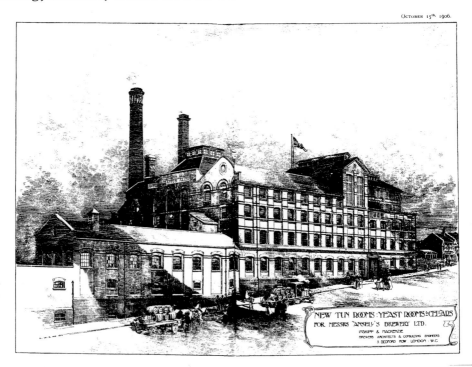

Extensions to Ansells Victorian Brewery.

Chapter 4

VICTORIAN BREWERIES

The Victorian era saw the expansion of the brewing trade both nationally and locally. This was attributable to four main factors – the rise of capitalism and the willingness of banks to loan money, the advance of steam and later electrical power, better transport systems, but above all, technical advancement. Coke was now used instead of

Beer labels from three of Birmingham's Breweries.

wood. Cast iron and copper replaced wooden brewing vessels. Cast iron mash tuns, combined with mechanised mashing, improved the brewing system, and cut down on the need of manual labour. "Sparging" or spraying the mash with hot water was introduced, replacing the earlier, and less economic system of mashing several times over. Temperature control proved to be the greatest advancement. Thermometers for measuring temperature, and hydrometers for measuring the density of liquids, gave brewers greater control. Thermometers allowed maltsters to produce paler malts that not only permitted the brewing of paler beers, but also ensured that higher levels of natural enzymes converted malt starch into fermentable brewing sugar. Accordingly less malt was required to produce more beer, thus maximising profits.

The 1850s saw the rise of two of Birmingham's three big brewers, Davenports and Ansells. Both had their origins in the malting and retail brewing trades. Robert Davenport appears as a retail brewer in the directory of 1829. His premises were at 120, Brearley Street. Joseph Ansell, started as the publican of the "Hope & Anchor" in Fisher Street, some nine years later. The Davenports expanded from retail brewing into malting and the public house trade. They bought the *Fox & Dog*" in Princip Street, the *White Horse*

Mechanised dray-carts at Davenports, c.1925.

Cellars in Constitution Hill and the *White Swan* in Hospital Street. In 1852, then head of the family, John Davenport, started malting at Bath Row, and the business was gradually centralised from here. Joseph Ansell moved to new premises at the junction of Lichfield Road and Park Road, Aston, in 1857. While Davenports expanded on their Bath Row site, Ansells began buying up smaller breweries. Among their early acquisitions was a site in Birchfield Road. In 1867 Joseph's son, William Ansell, joined the company. That same year the Bath Row firm became John Davenport and Sons. They are listed as maltsters, hop merchants and makers of Pale and Brown Malt for Brewing Bitter Ales and Porter.

Other Birmingham breweries starting up at this time include the Belle Vue Brewery, Handsworth, founded by James Horton in 1850, the Union Brewery in Mott Street, founded by Marshall, Allen & Dudley in 1851, Edward Cartwright's brewery in Snow Hill, founded in 1852, the Albion Street Brewery, Ladywood, founded by Matthew Bower in 1854, the Ashted Brewery of Thomas Smith, founded in 1859. Likewise there was William Hollister's Handsworth Steam Brewery, James Bate's suburban brewery at King's Heath, 1860, and Walker & Son's Birchfield Brewery, founded in 1863.

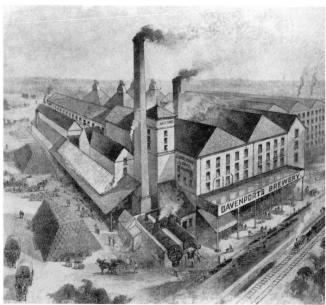

Left. A cartoon of Joseph Davenport, Chairman of the Brewery.
Right. A bird's eye view of the Victorian Davenports Brewery.

In 1869 control of the old 1830 law whereby anyone could set up a beerhouse upon purchase of a two pound licence, passed locally into the hands of the Birmingham Licensing Magistrates. They immediately clamped down on the issuing of new licences in an attempt to cut down on drunken lawlessness. With the street clearances of the Improvement Scheme for the cutting of Corporation Street in the 1870s, thirty-eight fully licensed public houses and nineteen beerhouses were demolished in this slum area. Their licences were not automatically renewed. Those remaining pubs began to soar in value. The brewers stepped in now, buying up public houses when they came up for sale. The "Tied House" system had begun in earnest. *The Brewer and Publican* (2nd. Dec.1892) reported:

"One of the most remarkable features of modern times is the development of the tied house system. As we move about the streets of Birmingham and other cities and towns we are astonished at the proofs of its rapid growth. A few years ago it did not seem a very great idea for brewers to buy up a few houses and supply them with liquors; but today this business is conducted upon a gigantic scale. In fact, the possession of public houses is now one of the chief aims of British brewers. From one

point of view the benefits to our towns is beyond question. Competition is set on foot in many ways. Owners vie with one another in their efforts to make their houses look as attractive and stylish as possible, and to carry out their ideas are obliged to call in the assistance of the various trades. For this they deserve the thanks of our Corporation and the public generally."

Despite this shrinking market, new breweries continued to be built. Former music hall proprietor, Henry Holder opened a brewery in Nova Scotia Street in 1870, John Dawber established the Mazeppa Brewery in Aston in 1875, Joseph Forrest established his brewing business in Winson Green Road in 1877, Henry Fulford established a brewery in Holt Street in 1878 and Atkinson's Brewery of Queen's Road, Aston, was also founded at this time. Some of these new breweries faced difficulties though. The Birmingham Brewing, Malting & Distilling Company, opened in 1878, was forced into liquidation in 1882. The Albion Street Brewery failed in 1876, but was bought up by William Henry Keel, and Edward Cartwright of Snow Hill took over the Birchfield Brewery in 1872.

Sir John Charles Holder, Chairman of Holder's Midland Brewery.

At the end of the decade two other breweries were established within a year of each other. Combined they were to become Birmingham's third big brewery. Henry Mitchell was born on 3rd November 1837, the son of Henry Mitchell, a member of Smethwick Local Board. In 1886, Henry jr, established a small brewery in Oldbury Road, Smethwick, but outgrowing it, he moved in 1879 to Cape Hill. Here he built a larger brewery with land beyond to expand. In 1888, the company was incorporated to become Henry Mitchell & Co. (Ltd.). The business developed quite rapidly, and in 1898 an amalgamation took place between it and Mr William Butler's Crown Brewery Ltd., of Broad Street, Birmingham. William Butler was born in 1843 at Hinckley in Leicestershire. His father intended him for the hosiery trade, but young Butler objected, and in 1865 he fled to Birmingham. His first job was in a hairdresser's shop almost next door to the *Crown* in Broad Street. In the evenings he worked there as a barman. He married Mary, the sister-in-law of landlord, George Owen. On their wedding day the couple moved as proprietors into The *London Tavern Work* at Smethwick. With the death of Owens, Butler returned to Birmingham, and became a partner with his nephew-in-law in the *Crown* in Broad Street. When the lease expired in 1880, Butler managed to secure a new lease at a ground rent of £840 per annum. The leases also fell due on a number of small cottages in nearby King Edward Place, and Butler managed to secure these also. Pulling the cottages down, he was able to build an up to date brewery on the site. Four years later, following continual development on the site, the plant and building were valued at £20,000. The business became a private company, and in 1898 the Crown Brewery merged with Henry Mitchell's Cape Hill Brewery to become Mitchells and Butlers. Production was moved to the Smethwick site, and though technically just outside of Birmingham, the company always styled itself as being of Birmingham. Before the outbreak of World War I they had swallowed up a number of smaller breweries; the Vulcan Brewery, Aston, James Evan's Brewery in Perry Barr, and in 1913, Cheshire's

William Butler, the Birmingham-based co-founder of M&B.

William Butler's Crown Brewery, Broad Street.

Brewery, next door in Smethwick. These smaller breweries were closed down. The object of the exercise was to cut down on competition, and to seize their licensed houses.

Left. J.E. Mitchell, son of one of the founders of M&B.
Right. A bird's-eye view of the old M&B Brewery.

A fierce battle had begun in the city, and indeed nationwide, to secure as many retail outlets as possible. The Birmingham brewery with the largest number of tied houses was the newly established Holt Brewery, founded in 1887. By 1890, just three years later, it controlled 155 tied houses. In that year the Home Office published the returns of ownership of licensed houses. (Parliamentary Papers 1890-91 (c28) LXVIII, p.2.). Listed opposite are the returns for Birmingham:

Butler's Crown Brewery, Ltd.

"CROWN   BREWERY."

ALES . AND . STOUT,
NOW IN SPLENDID CONDITION, SECOND TO NONE.
Awarded   Highest   Honours   and   Medal   for   Brewing.

OFFICES: BROAD STREET, BIRMINGHAM.

Advertisement for William Butler's Crown Brewery.

Birmingham (City of)

Holt Brewery Co. Ltd	155	William Thos. Rushton	40
Alfred Homer	56	Fox & Co.	16
Ansells & Sons Ltd.	64	Atkinson's Ltd.	16
Sykes Brewery Co. Ltd.	53	Flower & Sons	9
Showell & Sons Ltd.	40	Hood & Sons	13
Frederick Everitt & Co.	17	John Charles Holder	43
White & Lake	7	John Davenport & Sons	35
Wolverhampton & Dudley Breweries Ltd.	2	William Butler & Sons	19
		Mitchell's Brewery Co.	86
Hutton's Brewery Co. Ltd.	40	Threlfalls Brewery Co.	6
Ind, Coope & Co.	9	Truman, Hanbury, Buxton & Co. Ltd.	6
Mann, Crossman & Co. Ltd	8		
Brewers Investment Co. Ltd.	30	Executors of Peter Walker	10
Edgar Evans	3	Flinn & Co.	4
Pinder & Co.	6	John Hamilton Day	4
Edgbaston Brewery Co. Ltd.	3	Birmingham Town Brewery	12
Lord Calthorpe	11	Roderick & Sons	13
Sir Alfred Sherlock Gooch	159	Corporation of the City of Birmingham	25
Governors of King Edward's Grammar School	6	Ebenezer Piercy	13
Executors of the Rev. George Inge	12	Executors of Isaac Horton	14
		Fearn Guissley	7
Trustees of Lench's Trust	8	William Barwick Cregoe Colmore	20
Joseph Barrows	3		
Charles Montague Chester	6	Joseph Chadwick	6
Elizabeth Weidon	2	Charles Godfrey	2
William Jones	3	Lizzie Florence Moulton	3
Henry Edwin Jordon	4	William Brown	2
Jeremiah Howard	2	John Walker	2
Samuel Thompson	6	Frederick Chas. Arnold	2
Brooke Robinson	3	Alfred Rhodes	4
John Marston	3	London & North Western Railway Co.	11
Midland Railway Co.	3		
Samuel Marson	2	Mary Blanche Silver	2
Alfred Leadbetter	3	Charles Benson	2
Moses Tertius Collins	2	Harry Alfred Cope	2
Edwin Bingley	2	Cornelius Horton	3
Edward Wright	2	Mary Muggleton	2

Birmingham (City of) Continued

Walter Coleman	5	Benjamin Kelsey	2
Selina Howle	2	John Swann	3
Newsome Thwaite	2		

Included in Holt's 155 tied houses was the "Hop Pole" beerhouse in Lawley Street. It was owned by the Alcester Brewery of Church Street, Alcester, but was held by Holt's on a seventy-five year lease. A number of the licenses listed above were held by non-brewing freeholders of the properties, including Lord Calthorpe, Sir Alfred Sherlock Gooch, Birmingham Corporation and the two Railway Companies, London & North Western and the Midland Railway Company. Also included in this list are a number of outside brewing companies with toe-holds in Birmingham; companies that include Wolverhampton & Dudley, Threlfalls, Flowers and Showell's Breweries.

Showell's like M&B, styled itself as a Birmingham Brewery, with its registered offices at 157, Great Charles Street. The company was founded by Walter Showell, a Birmingham man. A former chemist and later bakery and beerhouse proprietor, he opened a small brewery in Simpson Street, Oldbury. Proving a success he secured a large piece of land including the historical

Left. W. L. Hodgkinson, founder of Holt's Brewery, Gosta Green.
Right. Holt's Brewery offices. Notice the painted sign on the wall.

The remains of the Holt Brewery, 2004.

Crosswell's Spring, near the Great Western Railway at Langley. Here he built his Crosswell Brewery, which opened in 1870. In 1884 the company became Walter Showell & Son. It was registered as a limited liability company in 1887, when Walter Showell handed over control to his son Charles, who then traded as Walter Showell & Sons Ltd. By 1890 the company had 40 tied houses in Birmingham, and with the acquisition of the Brewers' Investment Corporation Ltd. in 1894, gained a further 40 public houses within the city. Showell's Head Offices were moved to Great Charles Street, Birmingham, and extensive storage and bottling facilities were acquired near the Crescent, off Broad Street, with a frontage onto the Birmingham and Wolverhampton Canal. In 1914 the brewery, along with its 186 tied houses and 35 off-licences, were bought up by Samuel Alsopp & Sons of Burton-on-Trent. Brewing ceased soon after at the Langley brewery. The site was eventually sold off in 1938. The company, then known as Ind Coope (South Midlands) Ltd., went into liquidation in 1966.

In 1896 the Chairman of the Licensing Committee, Arthur Chamberlain, held a series of meetings with the Midland Counties Wholesale Brewers' Association with a view of showing how it would be possible for them to meet the wishes of the magistrates for the reduction in the number of licenses, without calling in the aid of the law or seriously injuring their financial position. The excessive number of licences in the city led to excessive competition, and this led to breaches of the law, bringing the trade into disrepute. By agreeing to surrender licenses, the profits lost would be regained by savings made in the elimination of rent, rates, taxes, repairs, till losses and wages. It was also put to them that as most of them were by then trading as limited companies, being seen to work with the licensing authorities would add considerable value to their shares on the stock market. The Brewers' Association agreed to work with the Licensing Committee. After selecting an area for inspection, all the licensed houses in that area were valued by an outside unbiased appraiser. Then the committee decided which houses should be surrendered. As a rule, the houses on the corners, and in the principle streets, were maintained. The owners of those public houses closed, in most cases a brewery, were paid the sum at which they had been previously valued. In this manner the houses of the outside breweries were seen off, admittedly with compensation. By 1910 there were just six non-Birmingham breweries represented in the city, and these, including Guinness, did not necessarily have public houses of their own.

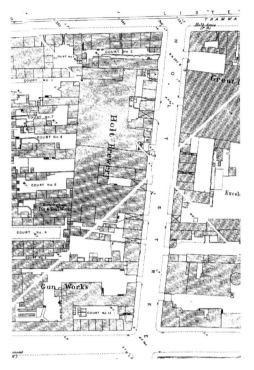

A late 19th Century plan of Holt's Brewery, Gosta Green.

SHOWELL'S

Indian Pale Ale in Bottles

AND NO OTHER.

SHOWELL'S Celebrated Ales and Stout in Bottle and in Cask to be obtained at these Bars.

Showell's Brewery Co.
LTD.

157, Great Charles Street,

Birmingham.

Showell's, though styling themselves as a Birmingham brewery, brewed their beer in Langley, in the Black Country.

Chapter 5

TAKEOVERS & MERGERS

There now followed a period of takeovers and mergers amongst the Birmingham breweries. Holt's Brewery, who had taken over Edward Cartwright's Birchfield Brewery in 1887, took over Grigg & Brettell's brewery in Sparkbrook in 1912, Joseph Forrest & Son Ltd. of Winson Green, in 1914, Kendrick Brothers' Engine Brewery in Brearley Street in 1918, Meade & Co.'s Wellhead Lane brewery in 1919, and the bottling company of Charles Heeley of Union Street in 1927. Ansells took over Albert Henson's East End Brewery in 1896. Rushton's took over King & Barton's West End Brewery of Wrentham Street in 1911, only to be taken over

The squirrel motif of Holt Brewery, later adopted by Ansells.

themselves in 1923 by Ansells. Managing Director, Harold Petit Rushton, was appointed to Ansells' Board of Directors, bringing with him 100 licensed houses. Lucas & Co. of Leamington, with 124 tied houses, and Frank Myatt's West End Brewery, Wolverhampton, were acquired in 1928. In 1934, aspiring brewery giants, Holt's, with 250 tied houses, were taken over by Ansells, who took their squirrel logo as their new trade mark. In 1952 Ansells took over the Leicester Brewing and Malting Co., shutting it down soon after, and using the premises as a bottling store.

Mitchells & Butlers acquired Cheshire's Windmill Brewery of Smethwick in 1914 and Birmingham-based Holder's Midland Brewery of Nova Scotia Street in 1919. William Butler's Wolverhampton brewery made a raid into Birmingham too, taking over Frederick Smith's Aston Model Brewery in 1955. Smith's, though they had 103 tied houses, had only 12 in Birmingham, with the exception of one, all of them were suburban. Of note was their *Fox & Grapes* in Freeman Street, a late 17th early 18th Century building, though encased in Victorian brickwork, and the *Royal Oak* in Lozells Road, a particularly fine example of a 1930s "Brewers' Pub." Butlers themselves were taken over by M&B in 1960. The previous year M&B had taken over Atkinson's Aston Park Brewery, who themselves had taken over Twist's Brewery of Walsall in 1950. There was even talk of Ansells and M&B merging in the late 1950s, but boardroom disagreements over the new directors scuppered what would have produced a near monopoly within the city, and inevitably the closure of one of the two breweries.

The third of the big three, Davenports, were also interested in expansion. Late starters in the takeover stakes, they acquired Dare's Brewery in Belgrave Road in 1961. With the brewery came 40 tied houses, chiefly to the south of Birmingham. In 1969 the Thornley-Kelsey Brewery at Leamington Spa went out of business. Davenports bought up their 29 tied houses, which again were outside of Birmingham. Brewery-takeover watchers at the time felt that Davenports themselves looked vulnerable.

FOR REALLY GOOD VALUE
TRY
RUSHTON'S 1/- IXL
FAMILY ALES.
LION BREWERY, ASTON ROAD.

Rushton's of Aston, extolling the virtue of their family ales.

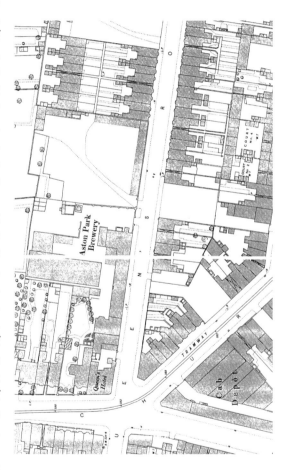

A late 19th Century map showing the site of Atkinson's Brewery.

Chapter 6

UP TO THE
MILLENNIUM & BEYOND

By 1970 the duopoly of Ansells and M&B in Birmingham was a fact. Davenports with only two public houses in the town centre, had ventured down other avenues, including bottling other breweries' beer. The "cosying-up" of the Breweries with the Licensing Justices back in 1896, had paid dividends. The two big Birmingham breweries were engaged in a unique system called Barrelage. In 1945 the Licensing Planning Committee devised a scheme to ensure that City brewers, whose public houses had been affected by war damage, or future redevelopment, should not suffer financially. Rather than pay them compensation, the Committee devised Barrelage. Under the scheme, before a new public house could be even considered for a license, the estimated trade of the house had to be calculated. The brewery wishing to open a public house had to state the number of barrels that the new premises would need. This was reckoned to be 2,000, at £10 a barrel. In order to obtain their licence the outside brewer had to pay either Ansells or M&B this amount. The then Monopolies Commission, had published a report in the previous year, criticising two cities, Birmingham and Bristol, for the abnormally high ownership of public houses by a limited number of breweries. Singled out for criticism were Ansells and M&B. Change was needed – a bigger choice for the drinking public was long overdue. It was not until November 1982 though, that Banks' broke the duopoly when it opened its first public house in Birmingham, "The Brook Meadow," in Shard End.

In 1934 Ansells began to redevelop their Aston Cross site. Fermentation wings, conditioning rooms, cold rooms and a bottling plant capable of filling 1,600 dozen bottles per hour, were completed before the outbreak of World War II. All building then ceased until 1951. The plans of 1934, designed to satisfy the company's needs for a generation, were "ruthlessly scrapped and replaced with schemes never before envisaged," revealed the author of an

Ansells Brewery, 1957.

article on the brewery that appeared in the *Birmingham Sketch* (Nov. 1957). Work to new designs, at a cost of £1,250,000, was completed in September 1957, the 100th anniversary of the firms foundation. The new brewery, one of the most advanced in the world at that time, covered a site of 4¼ acres. Ansells at that time controlled a chain of 1,500 tied houses, stretching from the Midlands to Bristol and the South-West, and to north and south Wales. Its assets totalled £22,000,000.

By 1961 Ansells controlled 2,400 licensed houses. That year they merged with Ind Coope Ltd., of Romford in Essex and Burton-on-Trent, and Tetley-Walker of Leeds, to become Ind Coope, Tetley Ansell Ltd., later renamed Allied Breweries. In September 1973 Allied Breweries put a further £2million into improving Ansells Brewery, just one month after investing £1million on new warehouse storage at the Aston brewery. The workforce, despite this investment, felt sure that Allied were going to close the Aston Cross brewery, in view of the apparent developing role of Allied's Burton-on-Trent companies. They staged industrial action in the Autumn of 1974, costing the company £9million in lost revenue. Further investment the following June, seemed to allay the rumours of closure. Allied announced that £30million

ANSELL'S

ASTON

ALES.

Advertisement for Ansells Ales.

was to be spent on refurbishing Ansells nearly 3,000 tied houses. At the time Robin Thompson, Ansells' Chief Executive, announced that, "it is the company's intention to ensure a viable and prosperous future for Ansells and the Birmingham brewery." Barely five months later, there was a strike at the plant when it was announced that without any negotiations with the workforce or trade union, certain beer-racking and distribution work was to be transferred from Burton to Aston. The six week strike cost Allied £7,500,000.

Amid a growing trend towards keg beer, Ansells announced the launch of a real ale called Ansells Aston Ale, in April 1978. It was launched from Holt's old brewery tap, now renamed "The Pot of Beer." One month later intended industrial action by public house staff was narrowly averted. Thompson laid Allied's cards on the table and announced that industrial action was ruining Ansells. The company also claimed that the brewery was now seriously over-manned. They decided to cut the workforce by 130, through non-replacement of those who

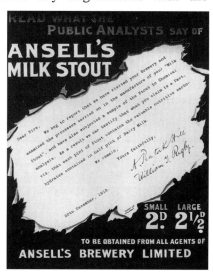

An advertisement extolling the purity of Ansells Ales.

A 1950s advertisement for Ansells.

left under a voluntary redundancy package. He also called for improved productivity. The following year 61 maintenance fitters struck because the company refused to pay them £5.60p a week for filling in for colleagues who were away on holiday. The strike lasted for three days before the fitters agreed to return to work while negotiations took place. At Christmas 1979 Ansells announced a campaign to get back to the days when Ansells had a stronger local identity. Old signage and styles were re-introduced. The reason for the change was that they believed a stronger local identity would appeal more strongly to drinkers than the corporate Allied image. Amidst a recession resulting in a drop in profits by 16 per cent, the workforce again went on strike in February 1981. Allied Breweries had had enough, and announced the closure of Ansells Brewery.

In May 1981 the workforce put forward the idea for a co-operative. The men asked to be allowed to continue brewing until the end of the year, and if they showed a profit, then the brewery should remain open. Allied remained adamant that the brewery would close by the end of the year. This sparked off further protest. In June the Transport & General Workers' Union Executive withdrew official status for the dispute. Three hundred and thirty of the workforce were found others jobs within the industry. The following March the site was put up for auction.

During the strike publicans had been allowed to buy-in beers from outside, giving the drinking public a choice they had not enjoyed for some eighty years – and they liked it. Meanwhile the original yeast culture which brewed Ansells beer, was transferred to Burton-on-Trent. Here they tried to recreate that distinctive taste. "Things can be added to water and things can be taken away," said an Ansells spokesman. "With new techniques we believe it will be possible to recreate almost exactly the flavour of the original beer." It was not to be however. The new mild with a distinctly pleasant nutty taste, was a very acceptable drink, and indeed it went on to win the prize for the best mild at the Great Western Beer Festival, but it in no way resembled the original.

Filling casks at Davenports.

Davenports Brewery, Bath Row, C. 1960.

Aston Manor Brewery was founded by four redundant Ansells workers, in March 1983. They acquired a former 22,000 square foot timber yard with buildings, in Thimble Mill Lane, and equipped it with former Ansells plant. A six inch bore to a depth of 330 feet was sunk, at a cost of £9,000, to extract hard water from the same water table formerly used by Ansells. Fifteen jobs were created initially, when the brewery began production at 100,000 pints a week the following April. Chief brewer, Phil Freakley, announced that Aston Manor beer would be a traditional cask condition ale with no chemical additives. With no tied houses of its own the new brewery found a niche market in selling plastic bottled beers to supermarkets and shops. It also secured a market for its cask beer in working men's clubs in the West Midlands.

By September 1983 the brewery was selling its ale through 17 outlets, including two pubs. Its first was the old *Ring of Keys* in Willenhall, renamed *Manor from Heaven*. New machinery stepped up production to 175,000 pints a week. The company also diversified into cider and bottled water drawn from the Malvern Hills and aptly named, "Malvern Spring." The following June, a policy switch saw Aston Manor selling off its then three pubs, *Manor from Heaven, Manor Born* at Brownhills and *The Cup* in Bilston, in order to concentrate on its bottle beer market. To further this, it produced a bottle widget, which kept ale fresh for up to five days after the bottle had been opened. By 1996 Aston Manor Brewery had an annual production of 15,500 barrels, and was employing 70 members of staff. Of the original four founders, only Phil Freakley remained.

Davenports who had for so long operated a trade union free brewery, recognised the T.G.W.U. as representing a sizeable proportion of their workforce in May 1974. This recognition and the sensible negotiations between management and trade union that followed, ensured that Davenports did not follow the destructive path of Ansells. In 1975 Davenports set up a canning line capable of filling 500 cans per minute. Among their outside clients were Fullers, Green King, Whitbread, Watneys Carlsberg and Guinness. The winning of a second gold medal in 1976 for the company's "Top Brew" instilled a pride in the workforce. Added to this was a turnover in profits of almost fifty per cent. In 1978 Davenports, who like many other breweries had followed a path of serving their cask beers under pressure, reversed their decision, and began returning to the more traditional beer engines. This followed on, when in the previous year, Davenports had been voted the "Best Real Ale in Britain" in a newspaper survey. In 1983 Davenports introduced plastic bottles for beer, and found an outlet through the Sainsbury supermarket chain.

Davenports success was keenly watched. In March 1983 Wolverhampton & Dudley Breweries made a £21million takeover bid. Finance Director

DAVENPORTS'

FAMILY

ALES AND STOUT.

Special Terms to Buying and Commission Agents.

BREWERY—BIRMINGHAM.

A Davenports advert emphasising the acceptability of beer drinking in the home.

Robert Houle, of the much larger Wolverhampton group, with 700 tied houses, announced that "it was too early to comment on whether any successful takeover would result in job losses." Such talk united management and men in resisting what was perceived as a hostile bid. Davenports' Managing Director, Neville Frost, announced, "We're independent and proud of it." On the 15th March Davenports' Board of Directors rejected the bid. Bob Houle commented that "the company is naturally disappointed…a board meeting will be called to re-think its strategy." W. & D. raised the bid by a further £3million, but this was likewise rejected. The writing was on the wall though for all to see.

An advertisement for Beowulf Brewery of Yardley. The company have now relocated to Brownhills, Walsall.

Over the next two years W. & D. acquired a 38.1 per cent stake in Davenports. Other breweries, notably Whitbread's, stepped in to ensure that the Black Country brewers did not acquire a necessary 51 per cent stake. Davenports sold off their famous "Beer at Home" business, in September 1985. As supermarkets mushroomed, home delivery sales declined. The company began streamlining its operations. By January 1986, W. & D. were on the point of acquiring a 45 per cent interest in Davenports. They put in a £32million takeover bid. The Board at Davenports were split. Drama was added to the proceedings when a bugging device was discovered taped to the underside of a table in the boardroom. John Bradshaw, spokesman for Wolverhampton and Dudley Breweries, expressed his astonishment at the discovery, and announced, "I cannot imagine who would stoop to such levels."

On 1st February W. & D. raised the ante by £3.5million. The deadline for this offer set by the Black Country men came and went. There was division amongst Davenports Board. Davenports Chairman was asked to ballot the workforce concerning their opinion. Unwisely perhaps W. & D. savaged Davenports performance figures and performance, and in the process alienated those in the company whose support they needed. Meanwhile Whitbread

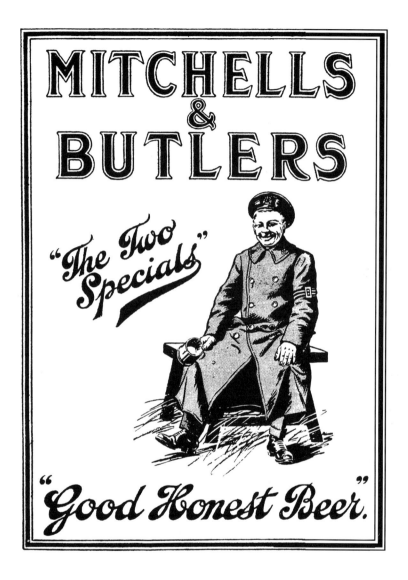

M&B advertisement, World War I.

Brewery expressed an interest in Davenports. On 12th February, out of the blue, came the announcement that Davenports were set to merge with Greenall Whitley of Warrington, following a £38million offer. Davenports Chairman, Charles Tidbury, said that the Board had accepted the offer after being given assurances "as to the continuation for the foreseeable future of brewing operations at Davenports Bath Row brewery in Birmingham."

The following year Davenports won first prizes in two sections of the Brewing Industry's International Awards. Their Continental lager was voted best draught lager in the U.K., while their traditional mild took top prize as the best cask-conditioned draught mild. In 1989 Greenall Whitley closed down Davenports Brewery, with a loss of 100 jobs, and moved production to Shipstone's Star Brewery in Nottingham. In September 1990, Greenall's announced the closure of Shipstone's, with production moved to Burton-on-Trent. The Davenport site was sold to developers.

It was refreshing, amidst brewery closures, to see the establishment of a new brewery in Birmingham. The Beowulf Brewing Company was founded in 1996, by Phil and Claire Bennett, with premises in Waterloo Road, Yardley. A microbrewery, it

"Deer Leap", a trade mark of M&B.

refers to itself as "Birmingham's only independent brewery," and now supplies over 300 free houses nationwide. It has three outlets in Birmingham and its suburbs, including the prestigious "Old Joint Stock" in Temple Row West. Beowulf's regular beers include Beorma, a pale ale, Noble bitter, which is very dry, Wiglaf a golden bitter with a malty taste, Swordsman, a pale bitter, Mercian Shine a hoppy pale bitter, and Heroes, a slightly sweet, golden nutty ale. In addition Beowulf also produce seasonal beers, including a summer wheat beer and a winter porter.

M&B, the last of the big three Birmingham Brewers, merged with Bass, Ratcliff & Gretton Ltd. of Burton-on-Trent, to form Bass, Mitchells & Butlers Ltd. in 1961. Six years later the new company further merged with Charrington United Breweries to become Bass Charrington. With 11,500 tied houses, the new combination was a serious rival to Allied Breweries. Far from being shut down, as had happened with other breweries, Bass Charrington planned expansion at Cape Hill. Not even a fire at the brewery

HIGHEST=CLASS

ALES

— AND —

STOUTS.

BREWERY—

CAPE HILL, BIRMINGHAM.

Advertisement for M&B.

in September 1974, could halt its expansion, nor a series of mini strikes in 1977. The pub tenants who had suffered in the strike, negotiated a sizeable pay rise, and were given a greater say in how their pubs should be run. In July 1982, £10million pounds was earmarked for refurbishing M&B's pubs. New houses, including *The Trader* in Acocks Green, were also built. In June 1987 a three year, £11million modernisation programme at Cape Hill was completed. M&B Chairman, Charles Darby said, "Much of the modernisation has been on major items of plant, making Cape Hill one of the leading breweries in the Bass group...It also represents an enormous investment in the Midlands." For its efforts M&B won one of five prestigious Business and Industry Environment awards.

On 18th February 2000, Bass dropped a bomb-shell – it was considering selling its beer making operations. Such a sale was to include Cape Hill and Bass's giant site at Burton-on-Trent, which had just merged with Carlsberg-Tetley, to make it the largest brewery in Europe. M&B's 400 employees were understandably anxious. On 15th June Cape Hill Brewery was taken over by Belgian giants Interbrew, best known for their famed Stella Artois lager, as part of a £2.3billion deal with Bass. The deal came less than a month after Interbrew bought Whitbread's brewing operations, which included Boddington's. With 32 per cent of the British market share in brewing, the Government instructed Interbrew to dispose of parts of the Bass empire. After some prevarication they did so, selling to the American brewing giants, Coors. Included in the package was the Cape Hill Brewery, which Coors announced was surplus to their requirements. M&B, Cape Hill closed at the end of 2002. In February 2003, pubs and hotel group Six Continents Retail, announced plans to continue running the chain of 2,100 pubs as Mitchells and Butlers.

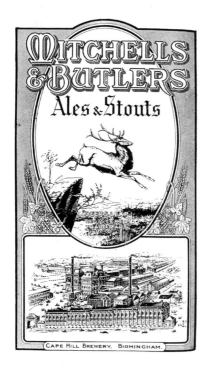

Left. Trademark and Brewery. Right. A pre-World War I advert M&B.

Chapter 7

A LIST OF BIRMINGHAM BREWERIES 1782-2002

ALBION BREWERY, Pope Street, Ladywood. Established by the firm of Silver & Ream in 1882. The brewery tap was *The George & Dragon* and the brewery was originally known as the George & Dragon Brewery. Maurice Silver was sole proprietor by 1883. The brewery changed its name to the Albion in 1885. Mrs. Mary Silver took over the brewery, following her husband's death that same year. In 1890, the Albion Brewery and its two public houses. were bought up by Sykes' Brewery Co., of Burton-on-Trent (part of Sykes Porter of Liverpool), who also had offices in Birmingham. Thomas R. Basnett was put in as manager, though his management was curtailed when the brewery was closed down the following year.

ALBION STREET BREWERY, Albion Street, Ladywood. Founded by Matthew Bower in 1854. In 1865 the firm became Matthew Bower and Son, with Frederick, the son, taking over in 1867. In *Hulley's Directory* for 1870, there is an additional entry for Matthew Bower sr., at Goode Street and Lodge Road. Frederick Bower is listed as owner of the Albion Brewery, and in addition in 1876, was also landlord of the *George & Dragon* in Albion Street. The brewery closed in 1877.

E. T. ALLEN LTD., *Dog & Duck Inn,* 180, High Street, Aston. A short-lived home brew house, registered in December 1918. Unable to cope with the stern competition of Ansells and M. & B., it closed on 23rd September 1921. The pub itself fell victim to redevelopment of the area in the early 1970s.

JOHN ALLEN, "Moseley Arms," Ravenhurst Street. Originally a homebrew house, taken over and developed by John Allen from 1854. He later became a common brewer and wholesale bottler. The business was taken over by his son Benjamin, in about 1890. The brewery and pub were acquired by Walker & Co., of Wrexham, and brewing ceased c.1900. Walkers in turn were taken over by **Atkinson's** of Aston.

ANCHOR BREWERY, Park Road, Aston. Established by William Trott in 1893. It was taken over by William Pickering in 1896. In 1907 the brewery was taken over by retail brewer John Stone, who had brewhouses at 92, Ryland Street and back of 58, New John Street. He had started in business back in 1882. The brewery closed in late 1909.

ANSELLS BREWERY, Park Road, Aston. Joseph Ansell, founder of the firm, started as a publican at the *Hope & Anchor* in Fisher Street in 1838. In the directories of the period he is referred to as a "maltster and retail brewer." In 1857 he moved to new premises at the junction of Lichfield Road and Park Road, Aston, and it is from this date that Ansells claimed as their year of foundation. Deep beneath the brewery site, seven artesian wells were eventually sunk, which pumped up 100,000 gallons of water an hour. In 1870 Ansell was joined by his eldest son, William, and in 1875 younger son Edward joined the firm, then renamed Ansell & Sons. In 1878 they acquired further maltings at 412, Moseley Road, and their expansion began. They bought up **Edward Cartwright's Brewery** in Johnstone Street, Birchfield in 1889. Work was begun on a new Aston Brewery in 1890, to a design by Brewery architects, Davison, Inskipp & Mackenzie. The firm was brought in to design further extensions in 1900 and 1906. On 14th June 1901 the company was registered as Ansells Brewery Ltd. Property and assets, including the Freehold Brewery, plant, casks, horses, stocks, loans and debts, including 388 licensed houses, were valued at £752,747. In 1911 Ansells took over **King & Barton Brewery**, and in 1923, they took over **Rushton's**, their smaller Aston rival. Former director, Harold Petit Rushton, joined the Ansells board. The **Holt Brewery** was taken over in 1934, making Ansells one of the largest breweries in the country. That same year they began building their new brewery at Aston Cross. William Jones & Sons (Maltsters) Ltd. was added in 1946 to increase production. In 1951 Ansells bought shares in Lloyds (Newport) Ltd., to enable them to expand into South Wales. During the post-war era the brewery was producing five bottled ales, Milk Stout, Strong Ale, Tonic Stout, Pioneer non-deposit and Pale Ale (matured in the bottle). Ten years later, in 1961, Ansells merged with Ind Coope and Tetley Walker to form Allied Lyons PLC, becoming the largest brewing

Ansells original 19th Century Brewery.

organisation in the world in terms of assets, with more than 10,000 public houses, hotels, restaurants and off-licences. By the late 1960s Ansells controlled more than 2,500 public houses. The 1970s and early 1980s saw a series of strikes at the brewery, and in February 1981 the decision was made to close the Aston Cross site and move production to Burton-on-Trent.

ASHTED BREWERY, 185,186,187, & 188, Ashted Row. Founded by Thomas Smith. It is first entered in the *Post Office Directory* for 1860. The following year the company was renamed, Ashted New Brewery. In 1866, George Wilkinson & Co. took over the company. In 1874 Wilkinson called in Birmingham architect, Edward Holmes to design a new Brewery, which was named, Ashted Steam Brewery. Six years later Ashted Brewery Co. Ltd. was registered as a limited company to acquire the business. Thomas Lane was appointed brewery manager. The company had a number of tied houses, including the *Apple Tree* in Dudley Street. The name of the company was changed in 1884, to the **Birmingham Town Brewery Co.** They ceased brewing in 1890.

ASHTON'S BREWERY (LATER THE OLD BREWERY), Moseley Street, Deritend. Founded in 1782 by Joseph Ashton, it was situated at the junction of Moseley and Alcester Streets. Ashton is the first recorded brewer in Birmingham, as opposed to a maltster. In 1786 James Richards became a partner in the firm, which was renamed **Ashton & Richards Brewery.** Ashton, "proprietor of the Brewery, Moseley Street, Deritend," as he is described in *Aris's Gazette,* died on 15th June 1787, and Richards continued on alone. From 1797 onwards, the brewery address is given as Alcester Street. On 28th April 1799 Richards died. His son took over the business and took James Goddington as a partner. The firm became known as **Richards & Goddington,** of Alcester Street, Deritend. While new rivals **Giles & Forrest** are recorded as "Ale and Porter Brewers," Richards & Goddington are not recorded as such until 1812; presumably not brewing the popular porter and stout until that time. In 1824 Goddington having died, Richards jr. continued brewing alone for the next three years. In 1827 Richards' Deritend Brewery merged with **Forrest & Sons** brewery in Warstone Lane, to become the **Warstone & Deritend Brewery.**

ASTON MANOR BREWERY, Thimble Mill Lane, Aston. Founded in 1983 by four former Ansells employees. They purchased plant and fittings from Ansells Brewery, which had closed in the previous year. Production began at 100,000 pints a week, with a staff of 15. The brewery became noted for its beer in plastic bottles, sold through supermarkets. At one time Aston Manor owned three tied houses in the Black Country, but later sold them to concentrate on their supermarket trade. By 1996 the brewery had an annual production of 15,500 barrels, and was employing 70 members of staff.

ATKINSON BREWERY LTD., Queen's Road, Aston. Atkinson Brothers Aston Park Brewery was established in 1878. The brewery was designed by Lancashire architects, Gregory & Haynes, who were brought in to conduct further extensions in 1885. In 1893 the company became **Atkinson's Ltd.,** and in March 1898, **Atkinson's Brewery Ltd.** At that time they had 80 licensed houses. City centre offices were opened by the company at 138, Edmund Street, in 1922, from where wine and spirits could also be purchased. Atkinson's expanded in 1950, with the purchase of Twist's Brewery Ltd. of Walsall. By 1955 Atkinson's owned 360 public houses. Nine years later, in 1959, they were themselves taken over by **Mitchells & Butlers.** Despite reassurances at the time by the Horton family, the then owners of Atkinson's, that there would be no job losses or closure of the brewery, M&B found it surplus to their requirements. It was closed soon after.

Atkinson's Brewery, Queen's Road, C. 1958.

ATKINSON'S

India Pale Ale.

MILD ALES.

STRONG ALES

FAMILY ALES

Aston Park Brewery

ATKINSON'S ALES.

Left. Advertisement for Atkinson's Brewery. Right. A beer label for Atkinson's stout, c. 1955.

Bates Brewery (later the Birmingham Brewery), King's Heath.

BATES' BREWERY, High Street, King's Heath. A small provincial brewery, situated behind the "Cross Guns." It was established by J. & J. Bates in 1831, and it is recorded that its water was supplied by an artesian well sunk to a depth of 1,1000 feet. The firm were brewers of ale and porter. In 1868 they became James & Isaac Bate, and in 1870, Isaac Bate's Brewery. The firm was listed as Isaac Bates & Co.'s, King's Heath Brewery by 1879. The brewery was sold to **F. Everitt & Co.,** formerly of the **Birmingham Brewery,** and renamed the **King's Heath Brewery.** At their height the brewery had thirty-five tied houses. In 1896 Everitt sold the brewery for £52,500 to Messers.Parr and Wright, business brokers. In March 1896, following a merger with it, and Messers White & Lake's **West End Brewery** and Albert Henson's **East End Brewery,** the company became **Birmingham Breweries Ltd.** Brewing continued at King's Heath, with production set at 33,000 barrels per year until 1899, when the company went into liquidation. See: **Birmingham Breweries Ltd.**

Left. The Greyhound, Holloway Head, brewery tap for Beard's Brewery. Right. The Lion, in Balsall Heath, a Beard's house.

BEARD'S BREWERY, 89, Holloway Head. Established by M.V. Beard in 1926. The brewery tap was the *Greyhound Inn*, which was later to become a noted cider house in Birmingham. Various members of the family were in the retail brewing trade, prior to 1926. Beard Brothers had a small brewery at the back of 39, Albert Street, near its junction with the High Street, from 1878 to 1892. James Abraham Beard had a retail brewery at Goode Street, at its junction with Lodge Road. M.V. Beard at Holloway Head, became Beard & Sons in 1949. They are briefly listed in the *Brewery Manual* for 1953-4. The Director and Head Brewer was A.V. Beard, the Director and Secretary, L.V. Beard. They ceased brewing in November 1965, when their premises were taken over as an outlet for Bulmer's Cider.

The rear of Bellefield Brewery, just prior to demolition.

BELLEFIELD BREWERY, 36, Winson Street, Winson Green. Established by Samuel White in 1897. White was a former jeweller, who about 1881 bought his first public house, *The Yorkshire Grey* in Dudley Road. He built a small brewery behind it, but wishing to expand the trade, bought the *Bellefield* when it came up for sale. In 1902 he acquired further premises at 217, Icknield Port Road. The firm became Samuel White & Son, in 1910. The street was renumbered in 1926, and the new address was changed to No. 40, Winson Street. Bellefield Brewery closed in 1951.

Bellefield Brewery price list c. 1910.

BELLEVUE BREWERY, Bellevue Lane, Handsworth. Founded by maltster, James Horton. It is first recorded in the 1850 directory of Birmingham. Owned for a period by Charles Maule. In 1880 the Brewery address was changed to Brewery Street, Handsworth. Bellevue Brewery closed in 1882.

BEOWULF BREWING COMPANY, Waterloo Road, Yardley. This micro-brewery founded by Philip and Claire Bennett in 1996, was Birmingham's only independent brewery. While it had no tied houses of its own, it supplied beer to 300 free houses, and is available as a regular in the Old Joint Stock in Temple Row, Birmingham, and The Bell in Tanworth-in-Arden. Beowulf produces six regular brews, as well as seasonal ales. In the summer of 2003, failing discussions with Birmingham City planners, the brewery was closed, and production was moved to Brownhills, Walsall.

BIRCHFIELD BREWERY, Johnstone Street, Birchfield. Founded by Walker & Son, in 1863. Peter Bough is listed here in 1866, but probably just as a manager rather than owner, because in 1869 the directory once more lists W. Walker & Co. Sometime during 1872 the brewery became the property of **Edward Cartwright** [See below].

BIRMINGHAM & NORTH WALES FLAGON BEER COMPANY. This company was registered in January 1905 as brewers, maltsters, hop and barley merchants, with a capital of £20,000. The directors were G. Ellis, C. Adams, G.G. Ellis and J.G. Bennett, who was Managing Director. By October the company had failed, and was in liquidation. The company had brewed beer during its short life; several barrels of which were unaccounted for, when the auditors were called in.

BIRMINGHAM BOTANICAL BREWING CO., 26a, High Street, Aston. Established in 1922. In 1925 it acquired further premises at Brass Street, Aston. It changed its name in 1933 to become the Birmingham Botanical Beverage Co. Ltd., of 2, Brass Street, Birmingham. The brewery also acquired premises at 118, Clifton Road, Balsall Heath. The Botanical Brewery closed in early 1934.

BIRMINGHAM BREWERIES LTD., King's Heath. The company was floated in March 1896. It was formed to acquire the **King's Heath Brewery,** the **West End Brewery,** late White & Lakes of Bristol Road, Albert Henson's **East End Brewery,** Aston Road, and 156 freehold and leasehold tied houses.

The purchases were made by Messers Parr and Wright, two of the company directors, and sold to the company at a considerable profit to themselves. As such the company being left short of money, was unable to pay either its debenture interest or any dividend in its first year. All production was moved to King's Heath, and the other two breweries were sold off. Matters remained in a fragile financial state, and on 6th July

A presentation card for Birmingham. Breweries, King's Health.

1899 the company went into liquidation. A court case followed, when investors tried to get their money back. The judge found that the brewery's "prospectus was misleading, but not sufficiently so to amount to fraud."

BIRMINGHAM BREWERY, Saint Peter's Row, off Broad Street. The brewery was originally known as the **Union Brewery**, and is shown on John Kempson's Map of Birmingham for 1808. The rate books continued to list the brewery as such until 1834. In 1814 however the brewery was taken over by a consortium of Birmingham business men styling themselves the Birmingham Brewery Company. An Indenture was drawn up on 24th March 1814. It recites:

THE BIRMINGHAM & DISTRICT BREWERY COMPANY LIMITED,

ST. PETER'S PLACE, BROAD ST.

BIRMINGHAM.

Presented by

Birmingham Brewery, off Broad Street, 1878.

"Whereas the town of Birmingham is very large, and the neighbourhood thereof very populous; and it is conceived that it would tend greatly to the convenience of the inhabitants if a public Brewery was erected to supply them with pure and wholesome Ale, Porter, and Beer of a genuine quality, and at a moderate price; and it has been proposed, and the parties whose names and seals are hereunto subscribed and set, have agreed to form themselves into a Company, Society, or Companionship for the purposes aforesaid, under the firm of the Birmingham Brewery Company."

As the indenture indicates, it would appear that the old brewery was either demolished, or extensive renovations and additions were made. Those gentlemen involved in the new venture included Theodore Price, esquire, Samuel Lloyd, banker, Sampson Tomlinson, merchant, Joseph Cottrell, gentleman and John Simcox, gentleman, all of Birmingham.

From 1821 to 1829 the brewery was known as the **Broad Street Brewery** near Islington. It also appears in *Pigot & Co.'s Directory of Birmingham* for 1828 and 1829 as **Horton & Smith's Brewery,** St. Martin's Place, Broad Street. During the 1830s and 1840s it reverted to its old name of the Birmingham Brewery Company of Broad Street. From 1854 its address was given as St. Peter's Place. In 1878 the brewery was renamed the **Birmingham & District Brewery Company Ltd.** The brewery closed in 1882. Its buildings were leased separately, including to other breweries as storage areas. The brewery was finally demolished for the construction of the International Convention Centre during the late 1990s. The offices of the brewery, a fine Georgian building, was spared, having been statutorily listed in 1978. The building is now known as the "Brewmaster's House," and is used as offices in connection with the I.C.C.

BIRMINGHAM BREWING, MALTING & DISTILLING CO. LTD., 257 & 258, Heneage Street & King Edward Road. Established in 1878, with offices at 27, Waterloo Street. Thomas John Williams, was its secretary. C.H. Thompson was appointed manager in 1879. New offices were established at St. Philip's Building, Colmore Row, that same year. The *Post Office Directory* of 1882, recorded that it was "in liquidation."

BIRMINGHAM STAR BREWERY CO. LTD., 58, Aston Road; 36, Holt Street, and 44, Mill Street. Walter Cheeman, Manager. A very short-lived concern, with no tied houses of its own. It was founded in 1889, but forced to close the following year.

BIRMINGHAM TOWN BREWERY – See: Ashted Brewery

BRITANNIA BREWERY – See: New Brewery.

CAMP HILL BREWERY, 58, Ravenhurst Street, (1933-45). Charles Herbert Morley, proprietor. It was a short-lived venture, failing to successfully break into the tied-house market.

CARTWRIGHT'S BREWERY, 86, Snow Hill. **(& BIRCHFIELD BREWERY).** Founded by Edward Cartwright in 1852, he is advertised as an ale and porter brewer, as well as being a maltster. In 1862 he opened up further premises in Summer Lane. By 1866 he had premises at 86, Snow Hill, 1 & 31, Summer Lane and 19, Cliveland Street, off New Town Row. In 1872-3 Cartwright took over **Birchfield Brewery,** in Johnstone Street, Birchfield, while still retaining his other sites. In 1880 Cartwright established his offices at 2, Summer Lane, but in 1881-2, apparently relinquished his other sites, transferring all production to the Birchfield Brewery. There are two entries in *Kelly's* Directory for 1886; Edward at Birchfield and a second Edward Cartwright, (possibly a son?), recorded as running the Cliveland Street and Summer Lane sites. In 1887 Cartwright sold his brewing interests to **Ansells.**

EDWARD CARTWRIGHT,

Wine & Spirit Merchant,

MALTSTER, BREWER, &o.

Wine and } 86, SNOW HILL,
Spirit Stores } 1 & 2, SUMMER LANE.
Malthouses } 31, SUMMER LANE, *and*
} CLIVELAND STREET.

SNOW HILL BREWERY, BIRMINGHAM, *and*
BIRCHFIELD BREWERY, HANDSWORTH.

Offices and Wholesale Department :
2, SUMMER LANE,
B I R M I N G H A M.

Cartwright's Brewery, taken over by Ansells in 1887.

CASTLE BREWERY, Prospect Row. Established by J.R. Downes in November 1893. The company went into receivership in November 1894, and closed soon after, perhaps without having brewed any beer.

CENTRAL BREWERY, Mott Street, Hockley. Founded by Henry Charles While in 1889. Additional premises at 18, Yates Street, Aston, were added in 1892. In 1900 the running of the brewery was taken over by Henry's son, John. In 1901 the firm became John While Alcock & Co. Last directory entry is in 1912.

Eli Christian's Queen's Arms Brewery, Highgate Street, 2004.

ELI CHRISTIAN, Queen's Arms Brewery, 278, Highgate Street, Sparkhill. A homebrew house formerly 31, Thomas Street. Brewing began in 1873, under Eli Christian. His son took over the business, then styled a "beerhouse." It became the *Queen's Arms* in 1936, under Thomas John Ashdown. The house was later taken over by Ansells, and in-house brewing ceased. A faded painted sign, proclaiming "Queen's Arms Brewery," was still visible above the doorway to the pub, until fairly recently.

CITY BREWERY, 20-21, Cato Street North (Formerly **Hutton's Brewery**). Established in December 1894. In 1900 the brewery site was partially taken over by **Holder's.**

CROWN BREWERY, 36-37, Broad Street, and 4,5,6,7, King Edward's Place. Founded by William Butler, it was here that he first produced his noted "Home Brew." The Brewery took its name from the "Crown Inn," a Georgian public house opened in 1781. The first proprietor of the "Crown" was William Taylor, who was succeeded by James Bloore, who in turn was

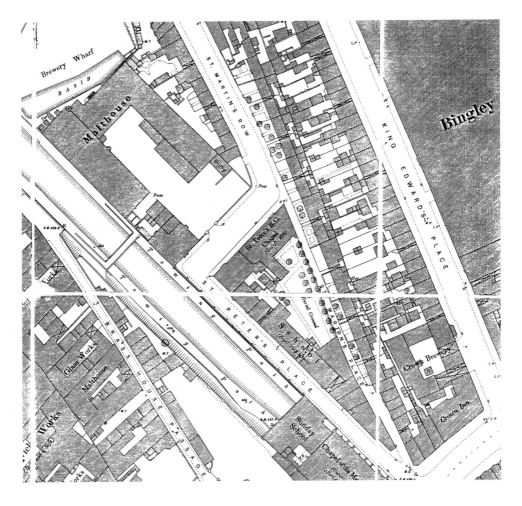

*A late 19th Century map showing William Butler's Crown Brewery,
and behind it the the old 18th Century, Birmingham Brewery.*

followed by Mr & Mrs George Owen. William Butler, a Leicestershire man, married Mrs Owen's sister, Mary. On the day of their marriage, Butler took possession of "The London Works Tavern," in Smethwick. In 1875, Butler became a partner with his nephew of the *Crown*, and manager on a day to day basis. Under him the "Crown" was reconstructed and refurbished to the designs of Bennett's Hill architect, Mr. William Jenkins. While at Smethwick, Butler had begun to brew for himself, and when the opportunity arose in 1880 to purchase twenty-five dwellings along King Edward Place, he did so. The buildings were demolished and Butler's Crown Brewery was built.

From the start Butler was able to brew 5,000 barrels a week, with storage for another 10,000, making it the largest storage in the Birmingham district. In 1898 Butler established another premises at 8 and 9, Old Cross Street, off Coleshill Street, Dale End, as **W. Butler & Co.** That same year Butler went into partnership with Henry Mitchell of Smethwick to become future brewing giants, **Mitchells & Butlers.** Beer continued to be brewed at the Crown Brewery until 1900. The Old Cross premises continued in use until 1931, when production was moved to the Springfield Brewery, Wolverhampton.

DARE'S SOUTH END BREWERY, Belgrave Road, Highgate. The brewery was established by William Dare & Son in 1903. It was registered as a private company, with assets of £75,000, on 29th August 1927, and became Dares Brewery Ltd., to acquire the business, together with other land and buildings relating to the old brewery. It remained a Private Company, with J.H. Dare as Chairman, W.H. & N.J. Dare as Joint Managing Directors, (N.J. Dare was also the Company Secretary), and A.T. Dare as a fellow Director. For many years their Head Brewer was William Glew. Dare's Brewery was acquired by **Davenports Brewery** in 1961.

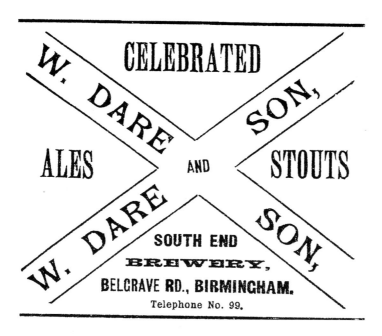

Dare's Brewery, Highgate, an advertisement of 1904.

DAVENPORTS BREWERY, Bath Row. The brewery had its origins in the early 19th Century. Robert Davenport is listed as a retail brewer in 1829, at 120, Brearley Street, Hockley, with further premises in Pritchett Street. By 1835 he also owned the *Fox & Dog* in Princip Street, and by 1845 the *White Horse* in Constitution Hill, and the *Swan* on the corner of Hospital Street and Summer Lane. Robert's son John, started maltings in Bath Row in 1852, and the business was gradually centralised from here. Artesian wells were sunk to a depth of 700 feet to provide clear sparkling water for brewing. In 1867 the business was registered under the name of John Davenport & Sons of Bath Row, maltsters, hop merchants and makers of pale and brown malt for brewing bitter ales and porter. Over the next few years the brewery expanded to fulfil demand. On 17th November 1896, Davenports Brewery became a limited company. By that time it had fifty-seven tied houses. In 1904 Baron John Davenport established their famous "Beer at Home Service." During the 1950s they advertised on television with the catchy jingle – "Beer at Home means Davenports." It brought in an extra 20,000 customers. The coming of the supermarket killed off a lot of this trade, and Davenports sold off the beer at home service. A second Company, Davenports C.B. and Brewery (Holdings) Ltd., was formed in 1929. This company also incorporated the Bath Row Bottling Co. Ltd. By 1959 the Brewery had more than 50 public houses, inns and hotels, as far afield as Wallasey, Leeds and Bristol. In 1961 Davenports bought up **Dare's Brewery,** of Belgrave Road, and in the process acquired forty additional public houses, chiefly to the south of Birmingham. Eight years later when the Leamington- based Thornley-Kelsey Brewery went out of business, Davenports secured their twenty-nine tied houses. In 1983, millionaire E.J. Thompson offered £24million for the company, but was forestalled when Whitbread bought up vital shares to block the move. Three years later, in January 1986, Thompson, then chairman of Wolverhampton and Dudley Breweries, offered £34million, for the brewery. It split the Davenport board of directors. but it too was rejected. On 12th February 1986, Davenports who then employed 1,200 people, including 300 at Bath Row, accepted a rival bid from Cheshire-based Greenall-Whitley in a £38.3million deal. On 6th January 1989, Greenall-Whitley announced the closure of the Bath Row Brewery and the transfer of production to their Shipstone's Star Brewery in Nottingham, with a loss of 200 jobs.

DERITEND & BORDESLEY BREWERY, 67, Alcester Street. The company was originally formed in 1840 by James, Haines and Turner. It is listed as Joseph James & Co. in *Shalders' Birmingham Directory* for 1854. In 1860 its proprietors are listed in the *Post Office Directory* of that year as James, Haines & Alldridge. In the directories thereafter the company is entered as either James, Haines & Alldridge, or the Deritend & Bordesley Brewery Co. Also described as maltsters, they closed in 1866, after twenty-six years in business. The building was later bought up by the Catholic Church, and the brewery was converted into a school.

DEVIS'S BREWERY, Bristol Street. Edward Devis opened a retail brewery in Ryland Street in 1845. He also operated as a maltster. In 1852 he moved his business to 193, Bristol Street, later expanding into the premises next door. The company closed in 1870, after brewing for twenty-six years.

EAST END BREWERY, Aston Road/Church Road, Nechells. The business was established by Albert Henson in 1891. The firm were listed as "wholesale brewer, wine & spirit merchant," in *Kelly's Directory* of 1894. The brewery was bought up by Mr. Ellis Parr, a business broker, and merged with Isaac Bate's **King's Heath Brewery** and White & Lake's **West End Brewery** in March 1896, to form **Birmingham Breweries Ltd.** All production was moved to the King's Heath site. The East End Brewery site was sold of to **Ansells** that same year.

A trade directory entry of 1845 for Edward Devis' Brewery.

EDGBASTON BREWERY CO. LTD., Wheeley's Lane, Edgbaston. Brewers of pale, strong and mild ales, the company was founded in 1887. W.H. Anderson was appointed Managing Director. The firm later expanded into wine and spirit shipping. Their town office was at 10,

The Staffordshire Joint Stock Bank Limited, Birmingham, and Branches, and Messrs. Barclay & Co., London, are authorised to receive applications for the undermentioned Capital.

The Subscription List will be opened on Saturday, the 18th of June, and will be closed on or before Saturday, the 25th of June, for both Town and Country.

THE

Edgbaston Brewery Company Limited,

BIRMINGHAM.

Incorporated under " The Companies Acts, 1862 to 1886."

SHARE CAPITAL £100,000 IN 100,000 SHARES OF £1 EACH,

MORTGAGE DEBENTURE STOCK, £30,000.

This Debenture Stock is to be created and secured by a conveyance and assignment to Trustees of the Freehold Properties referred to in this Prospectus, and by a Debenture Charge and Declaration of Trust, to be represented by Debenture Stock Certificates, and will bear interest at 5 per Cent. per Annum, by equal half-yearly payments on the 30th June and the 30th December in every year, the first half-yearly payment to be made on the 30th December, 1887, and is only to be redeemable at the Company's option on or after the 30th June, 1897, in whole or in part, at £110 per £100 on three months' notice, and is payable, if required by the holders thereof, on or after the 30th June, 1907, at par. The Debenture Stock will be further secured by a floating charge over the undertaking in favor of Trustees.

THE SHARES ARE PAYABLE AS FOLLOWS, VIZ.:—

5s. per Share on application, 5s. per Share on allotment, and the balance at two months' notice if required ; or the whole may be paid up on allotment, the Shares ranking for Dividends from the date of payment.

TRUSTEES FOR DEBENTURE HOLDERS :—

DIRECTORS:

FREDERIC CARNE RASCH, M.P., D.L., Woodhill, Danbury,
MAJOR BANES, M.P., Chestnut Lodge, Plaistow, Essex
REGINALD N. WOOD, Bignal End Collieries, Staffordshire.
CHARLES WING GRAY, M.P., Halsted, Essex.
CHRISTOPHER N. BAKER, Merchant, Birmingham (*Director of Humber & Co., Limited.*)

BANKERS:

THE STAFFORDSHIRE JOINT STOCK BANK LIMITED, Birmingham.
BARCLAY & CO., Bankers, London.

BROKERS:

SOLICITORS:

MESSRS. JOSEPH ROWLANDS & CO., 71, Colmore Row, Birmingham.

AUDITORS:

SECRETARY (*pro tem.*):

OFFICES:

Prospectus for the Edgbaston Brewery Co.

Temple Row, Birmingham. In 1892 the brewery's address was changed to Five Ways. Two years later, in 1894, J. Leslie Thompson became the brewery's proprietor. Former head, W.H. Anderson, with other interests, overstretched himself financially, and was made bankrupt in August 1895. The last entry for the company appears in the directory for 1898.

Bird's-eye view of the Edgbaston Brewery Co.

EDKINS & GUY, "Black Horse," Stratford Road, Sparkbrook. A home brew house founded by David Edkins sr. The brewery dates from 1859; the present "Black Horse" being added later in 1880. Upon David's death his widow Ann continued looking after the business until their son, David jr. came of age. David, also a brewer, went into partnership with Ann Mary Guy, a former barmaid at the pub. The partnership lasted until 1927, when Thomas Guy, Ann's son, took over the business. Brewing ceased in 1928 when the brewery and pub were sold to **Atkinson's** of Aston. George Frederick Williams was put in as landlord.

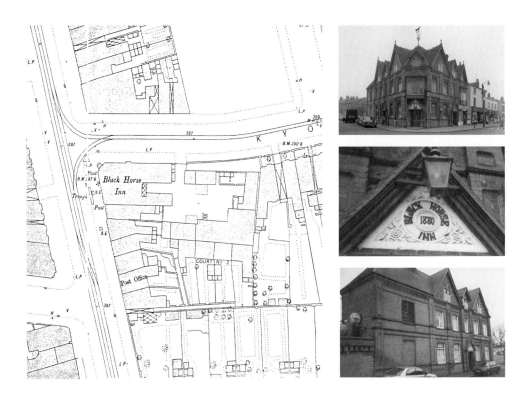

Left. The Black Horse, Sparkhill, brewery tap of Edkins & Guy. Right Top. The Black Horse, Sparkhill, brewery tap of Edkins & Guy. Right Middle. The Black Horse, rebuilt in 1880, as the brewery tap of Edkins & Guy's Brewery. Right Bottom. View of the old brewery behind Edkins & Guy's Black Horse, Sparkbrook, 2004.

ENGINE BREWERY, Brearley Street, Hockley. Established by the Kendrick Brothers, George and John Kendrick in 1901. Taken over by the **Holt Brewery Co. Ltd.,** in 1918.

FAULKNER'S BREWERY (later the **FALCON BREWERY),** Bath Row. Founded at 89, Bath Row by Benjamin Faulkner in 1834. Faulkner is also listed as a maltster. In 1845 the brewery address is given as 21, Bath Row, but this may be a case of street renumber- ing. In later directories the brewery's address is simply given as Bath Row. Faulkner died in 1853, and his wife Ann[e] continued to run the business alone until 1859 when she was joined by her sons. In 1860 the company was re-named the Falcon Brewery of Bath Row. Its life however was short. The Falcon Brewery closed in the following year.

FORREST & SON LTD., 192, Winson Green Road, Winson Green. Established by Joseph Forrest as a retail brewery, by 1877 the company had become a commercial brewery trading as Joseph Forrest & Son. In 1898, Joseph being dead, the brewery was run by his widow, Mrs. Ellen Forrest. In 1906 Forrest's became a limited company. The brewery acquired new premises at 9, Handsworth New Road, Winson Green, in 1909. In 1913 they were taken over by **Holt's Brewery.**

FULFORD'S BREWERY, Mott Street, Newtown. Founded in 1841 by John and Joseph Fulford. By the following year Joseph appears to be in business as a brewer by himself. Both John and Joseph are recorded as maltsters in *Slater's Warwickshire Directory* for 1850, the last year that Joseph is listed as a brewer. In 1852 Joseph was still at Mott Street, as a maltster, while John had set up in business at 1, Price Street, off what is now Lancaster Street.

Henry C. Fulford, founder of Fulford's Brewery, renamed the Holt Brewery Co. in 1887.

FULFORD'S BREWERY, 72-79, Holt Street, Gosta Green. Founded by Henry C. Fulford in 1878. Fulford was a former retail brewer at Acocks Green, between 1875-6. The family malting business had been founded as early 1819, according to the *Brewers Journal* (15th March 1877). In 1883 his business addresses are given as Holt Street and 152, Dartmouth Street. Fulford died in 1886, and the business was taken over by his brother-in-law, W.L.Hodgkinson, who reconstituted it as the **Holt Brewery Co. Ltd.,** the following year.

GILES & FORREST, Warstone Lane Brewery. The Brewery was founded by John Giles in 1786. In the trade directory of the following year the company is entered as **John Giles & Co.,** Porter and Ale Brewers, Whorston Lane (now the more familiar Warstone Lane in Hockley). David Giles, presumably John's son, was running the business by 1791, while just down the road **Alexander Forrest** had also established a brewery. Inevitably a merger took place, and the new company, **Giles & Forrest,** Porter & Ale Brewers of Wharstone Lane are recorded in *Pye's Directory of*

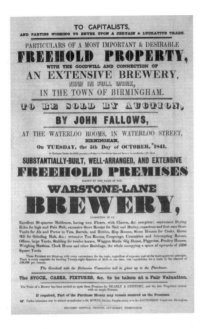
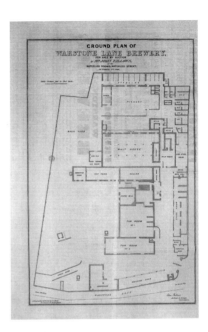

Left. Sale of Warstone Brewery, 1841. Right. Plan of Warstone Brewery.

Birmingham for 1797. Curiously Alexander Forrest kept on his old brewery until 1802, possibly to cater for extra capacity. In 1812 the Brewery was renamed **Alexander Forrest & Sons,** continuing as such up to 1828 when the company merged with James Richards' Deritend Brewery to become the **Warstone & Deritend Brewery Co.,** of Warstone Lane. [See also: **Forrest & Sons Ltd.**].

GRIFFIN'S BREWERY, Ruston Street, Five Ways. Established pre-1893 by George Griffin. "Pure home brewed ales. Families and the trade supplied in large or small casks."
(*Bennett's Business Directory,* 1902). No directory entries after this date.

GRIGG & BRETTELL LTD., Kyrwicks Lane and Montpellier Street, Sparkbrook. Established by Edward Knight, a retail brewer. In 1895 his brewery was taken over by Henry Grigg, who ran it until 1898, when he took on a partner to form the Grigg & Brettell Brewery. In 1906 they registered as a limited liability company to acquire the business. They opened a new office at Montpellier Street. In 1912, Grigg & Brettell was acquired by the **Holt Brewery Company.**

GRIGG & BRETTELL'S,

"COTTAGE" Home Brewed Ales, Wines and Spirits,

round the corner at the

"LORD NELSON,"

THORP STREET,

CHARLES MARSH, Manager.

Grigg & Brettell's home brew house, Leopold Street.

HANDSWORTH BREWERIES, Ninevah Road, Handsworth. The brewery was founded by the Hamilton-Day Brothers. They originated as retail brewers in Stoney Lane, Sparkbrook in 1883. In 1899 the brothers took over Flinn & Co.'s Ninevah Road retail premises, designed by London-based architects, Scamell & Colyer, and extended them before re-opening them as Handsworth Brewery. They also acquired Flinn's four tied houses. In 1901 the brothers closed down their Stoney Lane premises and moved beer production to Ninevah Road. J. Hamilton-Day took over control of the company that year. The firm closed down in 1912.

HANDSWORTH STEAM BREWERY, Grosvenor Road, Handsworth. Founded by William Dewdney Hollister in 1859. There is a directory entry for the company as Hollister & Smith of Grosvenor Road, Handsworth in 1863. Three years later, in 1866, Hollister went into partnership with the Thompson Brothers to become Hollister & Thompson Brothers. Three years later in 1869, the brewery was extended and renamed, the **Handsworth & Perry Barr Brewery.** In 1875 William Henry Hollister took over the business. He went into partnership with Joseph Chadwick in 1889, and the company's name was changed to Hollister & Chadwick. In 1892 the brewery, which by then had 32 tied houses, went into receivership, and closed in April of that year.

HIGHGATE BREWERY, 263, Moseley Rd., Balsall Heath. A home brew house founded in 1869, by George Eiton, a former retail brewer of Duddeston Mill Road. The brewery tap was known as the "Highgate Tavern." In March 1889, George's son, Edward, was found guilty of defrauding the Inland Revenue, brewing more beer than he declared. He was fined £50. Despite this he continued brewing until 1902, when he was succeeded by his son, John. John sold the business in 1906, when brewing on the premises apparently ceased.

HOCKLEY BREWERY, Nursery Tce., Hunter's Lane, Hockley. The brewery was established by Cox & White in 1833. They first appear in the Birmingham directory for 1835. By 1841 the partnership had been dissolved, and George Skinner Cox continued on alone. In 1845 a subsidiary company, G.H. Cox of Nursery Terrace, was formed out of the old. This evolved into George, Henry and Edwin Cox of Hunter's Lane in 1846. On 3rd April of that year, G.S. Cox, aged sixty-two, died at Bramford Farm near Erdington. His sons took over Hockley Brewery. In 1851 the sons sold the business to the partnership of Taylor & Cowell. George, Henry and Edwin Cox remained on site however, as the directory reveals, as maltsters, and no doubt continued to supply the brewery. In 1858, George Taylor, of Taylor & Cowell, took over the business. For some years after, his name appears in the directories, as an alternative to Hockley Brewery. This may be of no significance however, the *Post Office Directory* compilers may have preferred to use a director's name. In 1875 Henry James appears as the brewery's accountant, or "cashier" as he is styled. It would seem likely that Taylor himself had retired from an active day to day involvement in the company by this time. In 1886, the name Hockley Brewery is again used in the directory, though it is still under the management of George Taylor. The brewery was taken over by **Showell's Brewery** of Langley Green, in 1890.

GEORGE TAYLOR,
Hockley Brewery,
BIRMINGHAM,
PALE ALE
AND
PORTER
BREWER,
From the Choicest Malt and Hops, and Pure Artesian Well Water.

ESTABLISHED 1833.

Special Terms to the Trade. Private Families Supplied.

*An advertisement for the
Hockley Brewery.*

HOLDER'S BREWERY, 87,88,89 & 90, Coleshill Street. Established by Henry Holder in 1859, to supply his public house, the *Rodney Inn*, and adjoining music hall, *Holder's Concert Hall*, with beer. Holder opened his concert room at 87, Coleshill Street, in 1843. He extended the room to provide seating for some 600 people, which he re-opened on 24th June 1846,

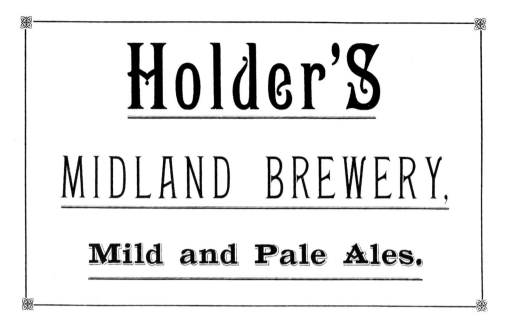

A somewhat discreet advertisement for Holder's bottled beers.

as *Holder's Concert Hall*. Holder sold his premises and moved to a larger site where he established a new brewery. The old brewery was taken over in 1864-5 by Gardner & Co. The enterprise was short-lived.

HOLDER'S MIDLAND BREWERY, Nova Scotia Street. Established by Henry Holder [see above] at New Thomas Street and Gem Street, in 1869-70, after he had sold off his public house and music hall. In 1875 Holder's son, John Charles Holder, took over the company. In 1879 new offices were established in Nova Scotia Street, and from then on the brewery address is given as Nova Scotia Street. In 1900 Holder's took over **City Brewery,** formerly **Hutton's Brewery,** of 20-21, Cato Street North, adding 40 more tied houses to their own 43 houses. Part of the brewery was sold off to **Vale of Evesham Brewery.** Both of Holder's breweries were

ALL OFF-LICENSE HOLDERS
SHOULD STOCK

HOLDERS

BOTTLED

ALES & STOUT.

SPECIAL:

HOLDERS

Bottled

Bitter.

"The Perfection of Bottled Beer."

A late Victorian advertisement for Holder's Midland Brewery.

run in tandem until 1913, when the City Brewery was closed down. In 1919 Midland Brewery was taken over by **Mitchells & Butlers.** It remained brewing up to 1923, when it was closed.

HOLT BREWERY CO. LTD., Holt Street, Gosta Green. Registered on 28th February 1887 as a limited liability company by W.L. Hodgkinson, to acquire the brewery business of his brother-in-law, the late **Henry C. Fulford.** The following year with Hodgkinson as managing director, the firm opened other brewing premises at 152, Dartmouth Street; 2, Summer Lane and Johnstone Street, Birchfield. In 1890 they became the **Holt Brewery Co. Ltd.** They took over **Grigg & Brettell's Brewery** in Kyrwicks Lane, Sparkbrook in 1912, and **Joseph Forrest Son Ltd.** of Winson Green Road in 1913. In 1918 they acquired the Kendrick Brothers **Engine Brewery** in Brearley Street. In the years that followed they bought up breweries in Wolverhampton and Lower Gornal. By 1930 Holt's Brewery had 250 licensed houses, including the "Old Crown" in Deritend High Street, allegedly built in the 14th Century. In 1934 Holts were taken over by **Ansells,** who also adopted their squirrel emblem. The brewery continued to function as Ansells No. 2 brewery until 1974.

HOMER'S VULCAN BREWERY, Park Road and Tower Road, Aston. Established by Alfred Homer in 1878. In 1882, the brewery added further premises at 77, Phillips Street, Aston Brook, and in 1884, 163, (back of) High Street, Aston New Town. In 1895 the brewery was shifted to a new site around the corner in Tower Road, Aston, just off Aston Cross. At this time they had 56 tied houses. Homer's became a limited company in May 1898, with a capital of £200,000. The Vulcan Brewery was taken over by the newly emerging brewers, **Mitchells & Butlers,** the following year. The site was sold off to H.P. Sauce, who still use it today.

A late 19th Century plan of the Vulcan Brewery, off Aston Cross.

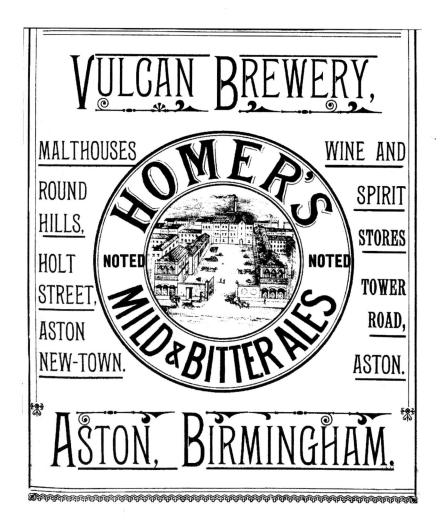

The Vulcan Brewery, Aston.

HUTTON'S BREWERY LTD., 20 & 21, Cato Street North, Nechells. Originally Hutton Brothers of Allison Street, being the partnership of R.B. and Thomas Hutton. The company was founded in 1881. Thomas retired, and R.B. Hutton moved to the Cato Street site in February 1890, where he established a limited company, trading as Hutton's Brewery Ltd. In March 1891 the company, which by then had forty tied houses, went into receivership. It continued to run until December 1894, when the brewery and its buildings, were taken over by **City Brewery Ltd.** (See also: **Vale of Evesham Brewery**).

IVY BUSH BREWERY, 226, Monument Road, Edgbaston. A Do-It-Yourself brewery, opened in 1994. Expert brewing advice was given to novices who brewed their own beer for domestic consumption. In 1995 some beer found its way into the free trade, brewed by in-house brewers. Demand never exceeded enthusiasm, and the brewery closed in late 1998. The brewing equipment was later removed from the premises.

GEORGE JONES, Station Hotel, Sutton Coldfield, 1868-72. A home-brew house, probably operating from a much earlier date, but not recorded in the directories.

KEEL'S STEAM BREWERY, 11-14, Albion Street. A short-lived venture, founded by William Henry Keel in 1876. A successor to the **Albion Street Brewery.**

KELSEY'S BREWERY, Henry Street, Gosta Green. A small brewery, established in 1889 by Benjamin Kelsey. It eventually had four tied houses within the inner suburbs of the city. George Kelsey took over the business briefly between 1913 to 1915, and was succeeded by his son, Benjamin, who ran the company from 1916 to 1934.

KING'S HEATH BREWERY, High Street, King's Heath. See: **Bate's Brewery** and **Birmingham Breweries Ltd.**

LADYWOOD BREWERY, 51, Friston Street, Ladywood. The company was founded by Samuel John Field in 1891. "Families & the trade supplied with home brewed ales" as *Kelly's Directory of Birmingham* for 1892 reveals. In 1901 it became Samuel John Field & Son. The brewery closed in 1912.

MARRIAN & CRACKLOW'S BREWERY, Heneage Street, Gosta Green. Established sometime after 1825, their ale and porter brewery first appears in *Pigot & Co.'s Birmingham Directory* for 1828. William Marrian, probably a son of the co-founder, also appears as a brewer to the **Warstone Brewery.** In 1838 Marrian & Cracklow's was renamed the **Ashted Brewery** of Heneage Street. John senior, died on 3rd June 1840, at the age of 74, and was succeeded by his son, John Rutter Marrian. In *Slater's Directory of Birmingham* for 1850, the firm is also recorded as maltsters. John Rutter Marrian died at Ventnor on the Isle of Wight, on 5th October of the following year, at the young age of 30. In 1854 the company became **Marrian & Co.** and the brewery was renamed **Heneage Street Brewery.** Through 1860-61 the firm was run by the executors of J. Marrian, but in 1862 the business was sold. It may have been acquired by **Thomas Smith**, who had a brewery in Ashted Row, which appears to have backed onto the Heneage Street Brewery. J. Marrian, of 245, Heneage Street, is listed in *Morriss's Business Directory* for 1862.

MAZEPPA BREWERY, Yates Street, Aston. Situated near Aston Cross, the Brewery was founded by John Dawber in 1875. It, and its brewery tap, the *Mazeppa,* took their name from Ivan Stepanovitch Mazeppa, a Ukrainian nobleman, who was reputedly tied naked to a horse as a punishment for an illicit love affair. In 1888 Charles Collins became its proprietor, but his tenure was brief. The brewery was bought up by the **Central Brewery** in 1891-2.

MIDDLETON BREWERY, Middleton Road, King's Heath. Situated just south of the village, it was founded by Manasseh Phillips in 1898. Little is known about it. The brewery closed in 1910.

MITCHELLS & BUTLERS, Cape Hill, Smethwick. Strictly speaking not a Birmingham Brewery at all. It is included because the brewery always referred to itself as being in Birmingham. The company was founded by Henry Mitchell sr. at the "Crown Inn," Oldbury Road, Smethwick in 1854. Henry Mitchell jr. built the Crown Brewery next door in 1866. During 1878-79 a new brewery was built at Cape Hill. By 1888 Cape Hill Brewery covered 14 acres and was employing 271 people. The company merged with William Butler's Crown Brewery of Broad Street, Birmingham, in 1898 to become Mitchells & Butlers. All production was moved to the Cape Hill site. The following year the new company took over Alfred Homer's **Vulcan Brewery** brewery in Aston and **Evans' Brewery** in Perry Barr. Cheshire's Brewery was bought up in 1913, and **Holder's Brewery,** and the **Midland Brewery** in 1919. **Atkinson's Brewery** was acquired in 1959. In 1961 the company merged with Bass, Ratcliff & Gretton Ltd., to become Bass, M&B Ltd. On 15th June 2000, the Cape Hill brewery was taken over by Belgian beer giants, Interbrew (best known for their famed Stella Artois), as part of a £2billion deal with Bass. With 32 per cent of the market share, the Government instructed Interbrew to sell-off part of their British acquisition. Cape Hill Brewery was disposed of as part of the package, to American brewing giant Coors. The company announced that Cape Hill was surplus to their needs, and closed at the end of 2002. The pubs still continue as M&B houses under former pub and hotel group, Six Continents Retail, who rebranded themselves as Mitchells and Butlers in February 2003.

JAMES MITCHELL, *Old Tree Inn*, 16, Hockley Hill. A home-brew house taken over by Mitchell, a former retail brewer of 5, Fleet Street. He offered to supply the public with home-brewed ales, wines and spirits. His pub had a quoits ground and indoor skittle alley. Mitchell ran the pub from 1860 to 1871, whereafter it appears to have been demolished when the area was redeveloped.

NECHELLS BREWERY, 340, Nechells Park Road. Situated behind the "New Inns." Founded by James Sandiford in 1875. In 1887 the brewery was acquired by Alfred Hood & Sons, who established offices and stores in Albert Street and Moor Street. By 1890 the Hoods had 13 tied houses in the Birmingham area. They changed their office address to Thimble Mill Lane in 1892. The brewery closed in 1905, after being taken over by **Holt's**.

NEW BREWERY (also known as BRITANNIA BREWERY), Walmer Lane. The brewery was opened in 1793. The announcement of its foundation stone laying ceremony on Monday, 9th April 1792, appeared in *Aris's Birmingham Gazette* (16th April 1792):

"On Monday the foundation for the most extensive Porter Brewery was begun by the side of the navigation at the end of Walmer-lane, in this town. The Gentlemen concerned, with their architect (Mr. Byfield of London attended on the spot, and the first stone was laid by Henry Clay Esq., one of the Proprietors, and late High Sheriff for the county – The designs for this building are allowed to be most elegant, and will render it the most convenient of any building of the kind in the Kingdom."

The brewery was served by the Birmingham and Fazeley Canal, and is remembered today by Brewery Street, which linked it to the present New Town Row. Curiously the brewery does not appear in any of the early trade directories of the town, though John Kempson's Map of Birmingham for 1808, clearly marks it as Britannia Brewery. There is an obituary in *Aris's Gazette* of 27th January 1812, relating to the brewery. It reads:

"Richard Wall of the Britannia Brewery, died 26th Jan. 1812."

That same year Pye's *Guide to Birmingham* describes the brewery as "the largest of its kind outside London." Jabet in his *Concise History of Birmingham,* for 1808, says, "The building is elegant and commodious, and was erected at great expense." The Britannia Brewery closed in 1818. The following year the premises were converted into a nail manufactory.

NEW TOWN BREWERY, Brearley Street, Aston New Town. Established in 1827 by James Boulton Oram, on what was then the northern edge of the town. Here the firm remained until 1850. They moved to Aston Road, and are listed in *Slater's Directory* of 1852-53 as J.& G. Oram. The following year, *Shalder's Directory* lists it as George Oram's Brewery at 6, Aston Road. However the firm moved again that same year to Scholefield Street in Nechells. Here they are recorded as maltsters as well as brewers. The following year Oram's ceased brewing.

PERRY BARR NEW BREWERY, Wellhead Lane, Perry Barr. Founded by Charles Meade in 1879. In 1900 the firm became Meade & Co. In 1904 it became a limited company. According to the directories they appear to have extended next door into the **Well Head Brewery.** They are not listed after 1919.

PINDER & Co., (Junction Brewery), 11,12,13, Dymoke Street, corner with Leopold Street, Highgate. Founded by George Thomas Pinder. He began as a beer retailer at 11, Leopold Street in 1880.

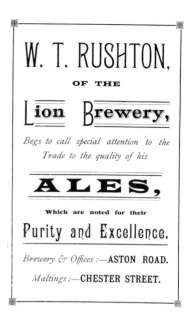

Rushton's, promoting the purity of their beers.

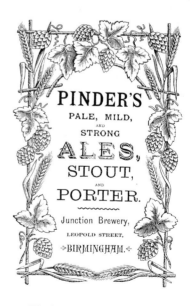

Pinder's home-brew house, Leopold Street.

Rushton's Lion Brewery, shown on a Late 19th Century plan of Aston.

Pinder became a common brewer in 1888, as Pinder & Co. Ltd. By 1890 he had 6 tied houses and off-licences. He advertised in a number of local magazines and theatre programmes, that he brewed pale, mild, strong ales, stout and porter. The brewery closed in 1892.

RUSHTON'S LION BREWERY, 69, Aston Road North, Founded by William Thomas Rushton in 1880. By 1890 they had 40 tied public houses and off-licences, including the *Old House at Home* in Lordswood Road, Harborne, a popular spot for half day holidaymakers. In 1892 they opened further maltings at the rear of their brewery in Chester Street, and at Clayton Road, Saltley. About this time they began producing their "Rushton's 1/- IXL" advertised as a family ale. The company was registered as a limited liability company on 3rd August 1898. Rushton's, situated just the other side of Aston Cross, was taken over by their near neighbours and rivals, **Ansells,** in 1923, following the death of their founder. At the time they had 100 licensed houses. Director, Harold Petit Rushton, was appointed to the Ansells board.

SIMCOX BREWERY, Harborne. Founded by Ainsworth Simcox in 1826-27. The Brewery had some unspecified connection, as the directories for the period indicate, with Barron & Slater's (**Birmingham Brewery**), Broad Street. In 1840 Simcox's Harborne brewery closed down.

SLATER'S BREWERY, Edward Street, Balsall Heath. The business was founded by Henry Slater in 1842, in Peck Lane. With the building of New Street Station in the early 1850s, the area, including Peck Lane, was cleared. With his evident compensation, Slater, then a retail brewer, established a brewery and offices in Edward Street, Balsall Heath. He also had a premise at 41, Severne Street, off Suffolk Street. The venture does not seem to have been a success. His last recorded directory entry was in 1858.

SMALL HEATH BREWERY, corner of Prince Albert Street and Talfourd Street. Established by J. Williams in 1901. Closed by 1903.

FREDERICK SMITH LTD., Aston Model Brewery, Lichfield Road, Aston. William Smith, born in Pinfold Street in 1819, and apprenticed as a cooper, obtained a beerhouse license in 1853. He named his new business, based at 24, Aston Road, "The Model Brewery." Two years later after extending his premises, he established himself as a wholesale brewer, supplying many of the publicans he had formerly supplied with barrels. In 1860 he bought two acres of land in Queen's Road, Aston, and built the *Queen's Hotel*. This hotel had a full wine, spirits and beer license. Beer still continued to be brewed at The Model.

Fredk. Smith's
Aston Model Ales

Noted for—

FLAVOUR
STRENGTH
AND
BRILLIANT
CONDITION

Aston Model Brewery,
BIRMINGHAM.
Established 1875.

An advertisement for Aston Model Brewery.

A late 19th Century Plan showing Smith's Model Brewery, Aston.

Between 1862 and 1863, Smith added a thirty-quarter malt house on his land in Queen Street, and in 1865 moved his entire brewing business to a purpose built new brewery that he had built in Queen's Road, alongside the hotel. Upon his death in 1878, **Atkinson Brothers** purchased the new brewery. Frederick Smith, then aged 19, went to work for them. Two other brothers took over control of two of the family establishments; Thomas the *Queen's Hotel,* and Henry the *Fountain Inn.* Two years later Frederick left Atkinsons and on 18th August 1880, purchased the **Victoria Brewery,** from its retiring owner, Tom Saull. Smith renamed it the Aston Model Brewery. In 1888, still under the age of thirty, Smith took over the lease of 6,000 square yards of land in Lichfield Road, Aston, and built a new and larger brewery, which was named the Aston Model Brewery. The brewery was completed in 1889. The new ten quarter brewery was designed by the Bristol-based architectural firm of George Adlam. In 1890 new offices and a private residence were built, and in 1892 a sixty-quarter malt house erected. The firm became a limited company in 1895, and a large number of public houses were purchased. In 1902, son Frederick Arthur Smith entered the business, and two years later he was joined by brother Sydney Silk Smith. In 1929 Frederick Smith was knighted by King George V for his public services to the people of Aston and

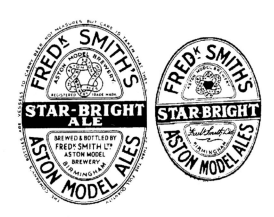

Beer labels, Aston Model Brewery.

Birmingham. In 1937 the company produced a history of the business, entitled, *A History of Achievement*. At the time of its publication the firm owned 103 public houses. [See Appendix A.]. In 1941 they bought up Albrighton Maltings near Wolverhampton, together with their licensed and other properties. The following year they took over the Castle Brewery, Tamworth, along with their licensed premises. Smith's in their turn were taken over by **W. Butler & Co.'s** Springfield Brewery, Wolverhampton, in 1955. All brewing ceased soon after.

ASTON ❀ MODEL ❀ ALES.

FREDERICK SMITH,

𝕬𝖘𝖙𝖔𝖓 𝕸𝖔𝖉𝖊𝖑 𝕭𝖗𝖊𝖜𝖊𝖗𝖞,

LICHFIELD ROAD,

ASTON.

Smith's Aston Model Brewery.

W. SMITH,
"GOLDEN CROSS,"
81, DALE END, BIRMINGHAM.

FOREIGN WINES AND SPIRITS,
OF THE BEST QUALITY.

Fine Home-brewed and Burton Bitter Ales ; London and Dublin Stout on draught and in bottles.

William Smith's home-brew house, the Golden Cross.

SMITH'S BATH BREWERY, 54-55, Woodcock Street. Founded by William Smith in 1876. It continued until 1886, when production was moved to the **Aston Model Brewery.**

WILLIAM SMITH, *Golden Cross,* 81, Dale End. A home-brew house. In 1866 Smith advertised in the Post Office Directory that he offered "Fine Home-brewed and Burton Bitter Ales; London and Dublin Stout on draught and in bottles." The site of the building was redeveloped during the 1960s.

SPARKBROOK BREWERY, Corner of Alfred Street & Ladypool Lane. Founded by William Terry in 1875. Taken over by the Hamilton-Day Brothers, who were known locally for their "Edinboro' Ales." The brothers later bought up the **Handsworth Brewery** in Ninevah Road in 1899, and moved production to there in 1901.

HAMILTON-DAYS'

BREWERS,

Sparkbrook Brewery,

BIRMINGHAM.

HAMILTON-DAYS'

Edinboro' Ales.

SPARKBROOK BREWERY,

BIRMINGHAM.

Left. The Sparkbrook Brewery, Alfred Street, Sparkbrook, founded in 1875.
Right. "Edinboro Ales," one of a choice of Sparkbrook Brewery's beers.

THE STAR BREWERY CO.,

Brewers & Hop Merchants,

CARVER STREET,

BIRMINGHAM.

The Star Brewery, a home-brew house in Ladywood.

STAFFORDSHIRE BREWERY, Johnstone Street, Birchfield. Founded by W.E. & F. Walker in 1874, next door to their former **Birchfield Brewery,** which they sold to **Edward Cartwright,** in or about 1872. In 1884, their last directory entry records them as William Walker & Co., Staffordshire Brewery, bottom of Chain Walk, Birchfield.

STANDARD BREWERY CO. 27 & 28, Duke Street. (1905-6).

STAR BREWERY CO., Carver Street, Ladywood. Brewers and hop merchants, 1895. A small scale brewery situated behind a public house.

UNION BREWERY, Mott Street. Originally founded by the partnership of Marshall, Allen & Dudley in 1851. Within a year Mr Dudley had left the firm, which continued under the management of William Marshall and John Allen. They are also recorded as maltsters, no doubt supplying the local retail breweries. The Union Brewery closed in 1858.

VALE OF EVESHAM BREWERY, 23-25, Cato Street North, with offices at 69a, Bath Row. Founded at Spring Hill Farm, Fladbury near Evesham, in 1895 by Ernest Bomford. In partnership with C.W.H. Smartt, he secured the **Old City Brewery** premises in Cato Street, Birmingham in 1899. In addition the partners also acquired large bottling premises in Bath Row. With Smartt acting as manager, all brewing was moved to Cato Street, from Fladbury, though the malt and hops continued to come from Evesham. The Vale of Evesham Brewery closed in 1906.

VICTORIA BREWERY, 192, Lichfield Road, Aston. A short-lived company, founded by Tom Saull in 1875. In 1880 Saull placed it on the market. It was purchased by Messers Roderick & Son, solicitors, on behalf of Frederick Smith. He renamed it **The Aston Model Brewery.**

WARSTONE & DERITEND BREWERY, Warstone Lane. Formed in 1828 out of the merged **James Richards' Brewery,** of Alcester Street and **Forrest & Sons** Warstone Brewery. The trustees were William Chance, Thomas Pemberton and Charles Bradley, formed together as Chance & Co. of Alcester Street. The two former companies continued brewing as Chance, Pemberton & Bradley of the Deritend Brewery, Alcester Street, and the Wharstone & Deritend Brewery Co., of Wharstone Lane and Deritend. In 1834 the brewery in Alcester Street was closed down, and all production was moved to Warstone Lane as the Chance, Pemberton & Bradley Brewery. The Warstone Lane Brewery closed in 1840. The premises were sold at auction by John Fallows, in October 1841, and the site cleared for house building.

WELL HEAD BREWERY, Well Head Lane, Perry Barr. Established by former retail brewer, Edgar Evans in 1878. Taken over by **Mitchells & Butlers** in 1899, it was still being run as "Edward Evans, Wellhead Brewery, Perry Barr. Ales supplied in cask or bottle. Tel. 146. Tel. Add. Wellhead, Birmingham," according to *Bennett's Business Directory* of 1902. From 1911 to 1919, Meade & Co. are listed as proprietors of Well Head Brewery. J. & R. Tennent Ltd., brewers of lager, are also listed at Wellhead Brewery, in 1915. Their business address is given as 70, Aldridge Road in 1916-18. Last entry for the brewery is given in 1918.

WEST END BREWERY, 110, Bristol Street (junction with Wrentham Street), 61½, Edgbaston Street and Smithfield Passage off Pershore Street. The brewery was founded by White & Lake in 1891. In 1896 they sold it indirectly to **Birmingham Breweries Ltd.,** for £22,000. The company was merged with the **East End Brewery** and the

King's Heath Brewery, to form Birmingham Breweries Ltd. The Bristol Road site was closed down when production was moved to King's Heath, and the old brewery was sold to King & Barton. King & Barton were themselves taken over by **Rushton's** Lion Brewery of Aston, in 1911.

The Edgbaston Brewery Company
LIMITED.

TRADE   MARK.

BREWERS OF

PALE. STRONG & MILD ALES,
WINE & SPIRIT SHIPPERS.

Brewery, Offices, & Duty-Paid Stores: **FIVE WAYS, EDGBASTON, BIRMINGHAM.**
Central Town Office and Sample Room: **10, TEMPLE ROW, BIRMINGHAM.**
Government Bonded Stores: *L. & N.W. Railway Warehouses, CURZON ST., BIRMINGHAM;*
and MILL STREET, WOLVERHAMPTON.

Advertisement for Edgbaston Brewery Co.

APPENDIX I

THE TIED HOUSES OF FREDERICK SMITH LTD. 1937

Albion Inn	Pensnett, nr. Dudley
Glasscutters' Arms	Barnett St., Wordsley
Albion Inn	Tividale Road, Tipton
Globe Inn	Blews St., B'ham, 6.
Angel Inn	Castle Street, Dudley
Globe Inn	Gungate, Tamworth
Bandon Arms	Mill Street, Bridgnorth
Golden Cross	Queens Cross, Dudley
Bassetts Pole	Canwell, Sutton Coldfield
British Arms	Colley Gate
Bird-in-Hand	Parkes Street, Brierley Hill
Bull's Head	Over Whitacre
Britannia	Pigott Street, Birmingham
Bull's Head	Pedmore Rd., Lye
Britannia	Hall Street, Dudley
Butchers' Arms	Fillongley nr. Coventry
Brushmakers' Arms	Cheapside, Birmingham
Copcut Elm	Near Droitwich
Bull's Head	Hagley Street, Halesowen
Crown Inn	Stambermill, Lye
Bull's Head,	Two Gates, Tamworth
Crown Inn	Friar St., Worcester
Castle & Falcon	Wolverhampton St., Dudley
Dog Inn	Nether Whitacre
Coachmakers' Arms	Stafford Street, Dudley
Gate Inn	Bourneheath
Crab Mill Inn	Oldswinford, Stourbridge
Gate Inn	Dawley Brook

Crown Inn	Lyde Green, Cradley
Gate Inn	Nether Whitacre
Dog & Doublet	Bodymoor Heath
Holly Bush	Belbroughton
Dog & Partridge	Loveday Street, B'ham, 4
Holly Bush	Hurley
Dog & Partridge	Cromwell Street, Dudley
Jolly Collier	Woodside, Dudley
Foley Arms	Pedmore nr. Stourbridge
Manchester Inn	Romsley
Fox & Grapes	Freeman Street, Birmingham
Maypole	Baddesley Ensor
Fountain Inn	Angel Street, Worcester
Model Stores	Queen St., Sparkhill
Fountain Inn	Portland Street, Walsall
Nag's Head	New St., Stourbridge
General Havelock	Alma Street, Wolverhampton
New Inn	Belbroughton
New Inns	Bourneheath
Royal Oak	Catshill, nr. Bromsgrove
Old Anchor	Worcester Rd., Stourport
Royal Oak	Lozells Rd., B'ham
Old Crown	Wigginton nr. Tamworth
Royal Oak	Park Lane, Aston, B'ham
Old Irish Harp	Mill Green, Aldridge
Royal Oak	Cradley Heath
Oliver's Hotel	George St., Tamworth
Salutation	Alma St., Aston, B'ham
Orange Tree Stores	Horsley Heath, great Bridge
Saracen's Head	The Tything, Worcester
Outdoor Brewhouse	Church St., Baddesley Ensor
Three Tuns	Lichfield St., Tamworth
Plough & Harrow	Mill Green, Aldridge
Vine Inn	Newtown Row, B'ham
Plough	Pailton nr. Rugby
White Swan	Kingsbury
Queen's Head Inn	Enville St., Stourbridge
Woodman Inn	Cattells Grove, Nechells
Railway Inn	Bromford Rd., Oldbury

49, Alfred St.	Handsworth, B'ham
Railway Inn	Forge Rd., Halesowen
Beehive	Bodymoor Heath
Ivy Cottage Inn	Catshill, Bromsgrove
Beehive Inn	Gt. Bridge St., West Brom
King's Head Inn	Mill St., Brierley Hill
Black Boy,	Heronfield, Knowle
Lea Tavern	Lea Hall Rd., Yardley, B'ham
Boat Inn	Ettingshall nr. W'ton
Nelson Inn	Hagley St., Halesowen
Brickmakers' Arms	Balsall Common
Old Crown	Toll End, Tipton
Robin Hood Inn	Collis St., Amblecote
Old Horns,	Queslett, Great Barr
Royal Oak	Wildmoor, Bromsgrove
Old Star	Sun St., Brierley Hill
Royal Oak	Dingle St., Oldbury
Old Robin Hood	Garbett St., Birmingham, 1
Samson & Lion	Halesowen
Queen's Head	Titford Rd., Langley
Star Music Hall	Walsall Rd. Darlaston
Queen's Head & Railway Hotel	Corngreaves Rd., Cradley Heath
Swan Inn	Fairfield, Bromsgrove
Swan Inn	Moor St. Brierley Hill
Railway Inn	Nether Whitacre
Swan Inn	Nether Whitacre
Railway Tavern	Trindle Rd., Dudley
Three Tuns	Walsall Rd. Willenhall
Red Lion	Park Lane West, Tipton
Unicorn	Orton-on-the-Hill
Red Lion	Walsgrave-on-Sowe
Whitehall Tavern	Whitehall Rd., West Brom
Rose & Crown	Reddall Hill Rd., Old Hill
White Hart	Walsall St. West Brom.
White Hart	Hurley
Wood End Stores	Hurley

APPENDIX II

WHO TOOK OVER WHO

Fig. 1

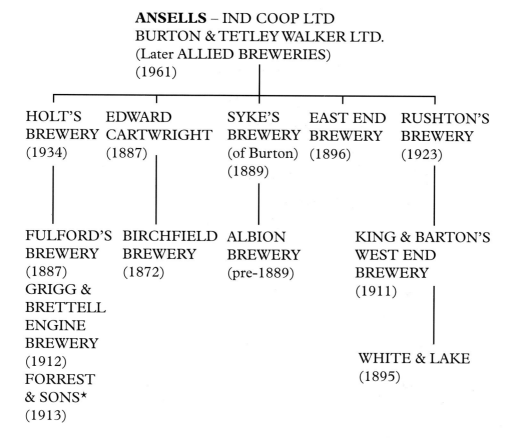

ANSELLS – IND COOP LTD
BURTON & TETLEY WALKER LTD.
(Later ALLIED BREWERIES)
(1961)

HOLT'S BREWERY (1934)

EDWARD CARTWRIGHT (1887)

SYKE'S BREWERY (of Burton) (1889)

EAST END BREWERY (1896)

RUSHTON'S BREWERY (1923)

FULFORD'S BREWERY (1887) GRIGG & BRETTELL ENGINE BREWERY (1912) FORREST & SONS★ (1913)

BIRCHFIELD BREWERY (1872)

ALBION BREWERY (pre-1889)

KING & BARTON'S WEST END BREWERY (1911)

WHITE & LAKE (1895)

★ The result of a merger between The Old Brewery and Warstone Lane Brewery in 1827, eventually becoming Forrest & Sons

Fig 2

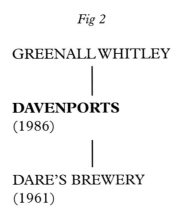

GREENALL WHITLEY

|

DAVENPORTS
(1986)

|

DARE'S BREWERY
(1961)

Fig 3

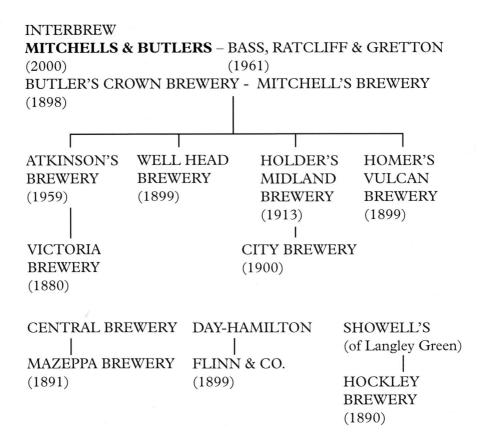

INTERBREW
MITCHELLS & BUTLERS – BASS, RATCLIFF & GRETTON
(2000)   (1961)
BUTLER'S CROWN BREWERY - MITCHELL'S BREWERY
(1898)

ATKINSON'S	WELL HEAD	HOLDER'S	HOMER'S
BREWERY	BREWERY	MIDLAND	VULCAN
(1959)	(1899)	BREWERY	BREWERY
		(1913)	(1899)

VICTORIA   CITY BREWERY
BREWERY   (1900)
(1880)

CENTRAL BREWERY   DAY-HAMILTON   SHOWELL'S
                                   (of Langley Green)
MAZEPPA BREWERY   FLINN & CO.
(1891)   (1899)   HOCKLEY
                                   BREWERY
                                   (1890)

BIBLIOGRAPHY

All material listed below is available in either the Archives Department, Local Studies Dept. or the Science and Technology Dept. of the Central library in Birmingham.

Biographical Newscuttings 1870-1930.

Brewers Journal, 1880-1930.

Brewery Newscuttings (LLF 66.51).

Chamberlain, Arthur, Licensing in the City of Birmingham: Birmingham Surrender Scheme. 1903.

Child, Samuel, Every Man His Own Brewer – A practical treatise explaining the art and mystery of brewing porter, ale, twopenny and table-beer. 1800.

Combrune, M., An Essay on Brewing. 1758.

Corran, Henry Stanley, A History of Brewing. David & Charles, 1975.

Directories of Birmingham, 1767-1970.

Encyclopaedia Britannica or a Dictionary of Arts and Sciences. 1771.

A General Dictionary of Arts and Science, or A Complete System of Literature. 1765.

A History of Achievement [Frederick Smith Ltd.] 1937.

Jabet's History of Birmingham. 1808.

Manual of British and Foreign Brewery Companies. 1899-1965.

The Owl, 1885-1907.

Mathias, Peter, The Brewing Industry in England 1730-1830. Cambridge University Press, 1959.

Parliamentary Papers 1890-91 (c28) LXVIII 1895 (c96) LXXXVIII.

Pictorial Guide to Birmingham. 1849.

Public House Newscuttings.

Pye's Description of Birmingham. 1817.

Rees, Abraham, Cyclopaedia, or Universal Dictionary of Arts, Sciences and Literature. 1819.

Richmond, Lesley & Turton, Alison, The Brewing Industry, a guide to historical records, Manchester University Press, 1990.

INDEX

N.B. Retail Brewers have not been indexed, as they appear in alphabetical order within the text.

A

Ale Conners, 1
Albion Brewery, 51
Albion St. Brewery, 28, 30, 51
Allen, E.T., Ltd., 51
Allen, John, 51
Allied Breweries, 40, 48
Allsopp & Sons, 35
Anchor Brewery, 52
Ansells Brewery, 27-8, 37-43, 52-3
Ashted Brewery, 28, 54
Ashton, Joseph, 5, 13
Ashton's Brewery, 54
Aston Manor Brewery, 44, 54
Atkinson's Brewery, 30, 38, 54

B

Barley Lane, 1
Bass Charrington, 48
Bass, M.& B. Ltd., 48
Bass, Ratcliff & Gretton, 48
Bate's Brewery, 28, 56
Beard's Brewery, 57
Belle Vue Brewery, 28, 59
Bellefield Brewery, 58
Bennett, Phil. & Claire, 48
Beowulf Brewing Co., 48, 59
Birchfield Brewery, 28, 30, 59
Birmingham Ale, 2
Birmingham & District Brewery Co., 13
Birmingham & North Wales Flagon Beer Co., 59

Birmingham Botanical Brewing Co. 59
Birmingham Breweries Ltd. 59-60
Birmingham Brewery, 9, 13, 59-60
Birmingham Brewing, Malting & Distilling Co., 30, 61
Birmingham Star Brewery, 61
Board Inn, 3
Boddington's, 50
Brewers' Investment Corporation, 35
Brewery, The, 5, 54
Britannia Brewery, 13, 80-1
Broad St. Brewery, 13
Brown Ale, 11
Bull Inn, 3
Butler, William, 30, 37

C

Camp Hill Brewery, 62
Cape Hill, 30-1
Carlsberg Brewery, 45
Carlsberg Tetley, 50
Cartwright, Edward, 28, 30
Cartwright's Brewery, 28, 37, 62
Castle Brewery, 62
Central Brewery, 62
Chamberlain, Arthur, 35
Charrington United Breweries, 48
Cheshire's Windmill Brewery, 37
Child Samuel, 12
Christia, Eli, 63
City Brewery, 63
Combrune, M., 7
Concise History of Birmingham, 13
Coors, 50
Coventry Brewery, 13
Crosswell Brewery, 35

Crown Brewery, 30, 63-5
Crown Inn, Broad St., 31
Cup, The, 45

D
Darby, Charles, 49
Dare's Brewery, 38, 65
Davenports Brewery, 27-8, 38, 45-8, 66
DeBermingham, Edward, 2
Deritend & Bordesley Brewery, 66-7
Devis's Brewery, 67
Digbeth Mineral Springs Co., 2

E
East End Brewery, 37, 67
Edgbaston Brewery, 67-8
Edkins & Guy, 69-70
Engine Brewery, 37, 70
Entire Butt, 6
Essay on Brewing, 7
Evans Brewery, 31
Every Man His Own Brewer, 12

F
Falcon Brewery, 70
Faulkner's Brewery, 70
Forrest & Sons, 7-8, 13, 37, 71
Forrest Joseph, 30
Fox & Dog, 27
Fox & Grapes, 38
Freakley, Phil., 44-5
Frost, Neville, 46
Fulford, Henry, 30
Fuller's Brewery, 45, 71

G
Giles & Co., 6
Giles & Forrest, 71
God Welle feld, 1
Green King Brewery, 45
Greenall-Whitley Brewery, 47-8
Griffin's Brewery, 72
Grigg & Brettell's Brewery, 13, 37, 72
Guinness, 36, 45

H
Handsworth Breweries, 73
Handsworth Steam Brewery, 28, 73
Harwood, Ralph, 6
Heeley, Charles, 37
Highgate Brewery, 73
Hockley Brewery, 74
Hoffmeyer, John, 14
Holder, Henry, 30
Holder's Midland Brewery, 37, 75
Hollister, William, 28
Holt Brewery, 32, 37, 41, 76
Homer's Vulcan Brewery, 36, 76
Hop Pole, 34
Hope & Anchor, 27
Hutton's Brewery Ltd., 77

I
Improvement Scheme, 29
Ind Coop Ltd., 40
Interbrew, 50
Ivy Bush Brewery, 78

J
Jones, George, 78

K
Keel's Steam Brewery, 78
Kelsey's Brewery, 78
King & Barton, 37

L
Ladywood Brewery, 78
Leicester Brewing & Malting Co., 37
Lloyd, David, 13
Lloyd, Samuel, 13
London & County Brewer, 4
London Tavern, 31

M
M. & B., 37-8, 39, 48-50, 79-80
Maiden Head Inn, 3
Malvern Spring, 44
Manor Born, 45
Manor from Heaven, 44

Marrian & Cracklow's Brewery, 78
Mazeppa Brewery 30, 79
Midland Counties Wholesale Brewers'
  Assoc., 35-6
Middleton Brewery, 79
Mitchell, Henry, 30-1
Mitchell, James, 80
Myatt, Frank, 37

N
Nechells Brewery, 80
New Brewery, 80-1
New Town Brewery, 81

O
Old Joint Stock, 48
Owen, George, 31

P
Pale Ale, 12
Perry Barr New Brewery, 81
Pinder & Co., 81-2
Porter, 9-11
Pot of Beer, 41
Priory of St. Thomas, 2

R
Red Lion, 3
Reindeer Inn, 3
Richards & Co., 13
Richards & Goddington, 13
Ring of Keys, 44
Royal Oak, 38
Rushton, Harold P., 37
Rushton's Brewery, 37, 82-3

S
Shipstone's Brewery, 48
Showell, Walter, 34-5
Showell's Brewery, 34
Simcox Brewery, 83
Six Continents Retail, 50
Small Heath Brewery, 83
Smith's Aston Model Brewery, 37, 83-5,
  90-2

Smith's Bath Brewery, 86
Smith, William, 86
"Sparging", 27
Sparkbrook Brewery, 86
Staffordshire Brewery, 87
Staler's Brewery, 83
Standard Brewery, 87
Star Brewery, 87
Stella Artois, 50
Stout, 9-11
Swan Inn, 3

T
Tetley Walker, 40
Thornley-Kelsey Brewery, 38
Tied House System, 29-30
Trader, The, 49
Twist's Brewery, 38

U
Union Brewery, 13, 28, 87

V
Vale Of Evesham Brewery, 87
Victoria Brewery, 88
Vulcan Brewery, 31, 76

W
Warstone Brewery, 7-8
Warstone & Deritend Brewery, 88
Watney's Brewery, 45
Wellington's Beer House Act, 13
Wellhead Lane Brewery, 37, 88
West End Brewery, 37, 88
Westley's Plan of Birmingham, 2
Whitbread Brewery, 45-46, 50
White Hart, 3
White Horse Cellars, 27
White Swan, 28
Wolverhampton & Dudley Breweries, 45-6